Rational expectations and monetary policy

Rational expectations and monetary policy

J. J. SIJBEN

Tilburg University, Tilburg, The Netherlands

SIJTHOFF & NOORDHOFF 1980
Alphen aan den Rijn, The Netherlands
Germantown, Maryland USA

ISBN 90 286 0030 2

Library of Congress Catalog Card Number: 79-56565

Printed in The Netherlands

Table of contents

List of symbols

B	monetary base
R	reserves of commercial banks
C	currency in circulation
D	demand deposits
T	time deposits
E	excess reserves of commercial banks
M	money supply
r^d	reserve percentage of demand deposit liabilities
r^t	reserve percentage of time deposit liabilities
c	ratio of currency to private demand deposits
t	ratio of time deposits to private demand deposits
e	ratio of excess reserves to demand deposits
X	excess demand on the goods and labour market
U_N	natural rate of unemployment
U_F	actual rate of unemployment
π	actual rate of inflation
π^*	expected rate of inflation
m	actual rate of monetary growth
m^*	expected rate of monetary growth
W	money wage rate
P	price level
l^d	labour demand
l^s	labour supply
l	employment
l^*	labour market equilibrium
α	price expectations coefficient
γ	trade-off parameter
$\dot{\pi}$	acceleration of the rate of inflation
λ	adjustment coefficient
ε	error term in inflation equation
μ	error term in anticyclical money supply rule
E	mathematical expectations
I	information set
ψ	reaction parameter
β	reaction parameter
ρ	error term in the aggregate supply function
$\dot{y}$	rate of growth of real output
y	real output

Preface

The last few years a growing interest could be observed for "monetarist" thinking, i.e. the idea that for controlling the price level, that means the stabilization of the value of money, a great importance should be attributed to the control of the growth of the money supply or of the quantity of liquid assets.

These rather recent visions, which were first defended in the United States and later in Europe, suggest that a real monetary policy in the sense of a regular tuning by monetary authorities is not feasible but that it is better to limit the growth of the money supply or some other monetary aggregate by a yearly percentage which should be maintained as stable as possible.

These ideas look at first view rather simplistic when looking at our complicated Western society. But further study reveals that this approach is based on certain assumptions concerning the expectation pattern of households and enterprises. The author of this book does not only attempt to give a review of the monetarist theory of which there are of course different variants, but he deals explicitly and extensively with the assumptions that are behind these variants.

Dr. Sijben is an economist who is very able to fulfill this task: his thesis "Money and economic growth" (1977) showed his great knowledge of the very extensive literature in this field. But the study that is now being published is of special importance in that it explains the underlying assumptions of the expectations theory so clearly, extensively and without omitting any necessary link.

As I said before the monetarist theories are becoming more and more relevant: in the Federal Republic of Germany monetary policy as it is implemented is based on a concept related to the monetarist one. There is a "Shadow European Economic Policy Committee", consisting of eminent economists that judges economic policy in the most important countries from the monetarist point of view.

This means that it is imperative for everyone who, in theory or in practice, has to deal with economic policy, to get acquainted with this school of thought. Reading Dr. Sijben's new book will elucidate what was before unclear or only understood in rather vague terms.

Dr. H. W. J. Bosman
Professor of Money and Banking
Tilburg University, Tilburg,
The Netherlands

1. General introduction

Since the early seventies macroeconomic stabilization policy has been strongly emphasized in the theoretical literature on monetary economics, especially in regard to the elimination of the phenomena of inflation and unemployment. This attention has arisen because inflationary expectations and the concomitant catching-up and leapfrogging in price and wage adjustments have a substantial impact on the ultimate course of the economic process. However one of the most difficult problems confronting the scientist in macroeconomic model building is the indication and description of the mechanism by which economic agents make up their expectations of certain strategic economic variables in the future, for the crucial behaviour-equations in macroeconomic models are essentially based on suppositions concerning the mechanism which moulds the expectations of the relevant economic variables. The critical importance of this expectations mechanism in the development of the general price level was clearly demonstrated in the last decade in the literature on monetary growth theory and in Phelps's analysis on the microeconomic foundations of the inflation problem (Sijben 1977, chs. 3, 4; Phelps 1970).

In the last decade, and especially since the early seventies, some American economists in the field of macroeconomic theory (Lucas, Sargent, Wallace) have developed a theoretical framework which has quite far-reaching consequences in conducting economic policy, in particular with respect to monetary policy. This school of thought within the monetarist camp, known as the "rationalists", can be considered as a continuation of the Keynesian revolution of the thirties, and of

Friedman's monetary counter-revolution in the fifties.

The nucleus of their theoretical views essentially regards the economic policymakers as being unable to implement a systematic anticyclical economic policy (activism) to stabilize employment and to achieve a target of real national income. In this respect this theory can be seen as a revolution in the development of macroeconomic theory. Tightly interconnected in this theory are the expectations procedures of economic agents in building up their expectations of the rate of inflation, the rate of interest, the foreign exchange rate, and so on. The macroeconomic theorists mentioned above assume that the public builds up its expectations rationally, and therein makes use of all the available relevant information about the variables, which, according to the economic theory, determine the development of the economic variable to be predicted. In these circumstances expectations are endogenous to the model and the subjective predictions of the values of the relevant economic variables will not deviate systematically from the outcomes generated by the theoretical model of the economy. This results from the fact that economic relations according to the model are essentially the basis of the expectations mechanism of the public. Further, the "rationalists" point out, only random and unexpected monetary impulses and demand-pulls, which surprise the economic agents so that they cannot adjust their economic behaviour immediately, will have an impact on the real variables, that is, on production and employment. Economic policy measures only generate a substantial influence on the real sector of the economy insofar as the expectations structure of the economic agents will be changed. However a systematic monetary policy implementation mitigating the fluctuations in economic activity will be doomed to failure in the long run, because economic agents will anticipate this policy after a learning period and will adjust their economic decisions appropriately. In this way the economy appears to be resistant to an activism in economic policy (Lucas 1973; Sargent and Wallace 1976; Barro 1976). The influence of the "rationalists", who proclaim the end of the Keynesian era and who would abandon Keynesian stabilization policy, is growing steadily also with respect to the development of macroeconomic theory. Sargent observes, "The raw fact that hits everybody is that the economy has just not behaved according to the best Keynesian models. We were good Keynesians once, but we have to change our minds" (*Newsweek* 1978, p. 35). We intend to review in this study the present state of the rational expectations hypothesis and its impact on the effectiveness of monetary policy, as it appears from the recent literature.

The second chapter of this study presents a detailed exposition of the crucial controversial issues dividing monetarists and non-monetarists, with regard to the theoretical foundations of monetary policy as these are presented in postwar economic literature. These issues arise from the attack on Keynesian views begun in the sixties by the monetarist camp, who attracted special attention to the conflicts between Keynesians (non-monetarists) and monetarists. In Chapters 3 to 6 attention will be paid to the different processes according to which inflationary expectations are built up and to the consequences of these expectations procedures for the effectiveness of macroeconomic stabilization policy and especially with regard to monetary policy. In Chapter 3 a short historical review of some important viewpoints existing in the economic literature concerning the question of the formation of expectations of economic variables will be presented. In this context two schools of thought can be distinguished: on the one side the theory of adaptive or auto-regressive expectations, and the rational-expectations hypothesis on the other side. Chapter 4 contains an exposition of the influence of the endogenization of inflation expectations on the well-known policy dilemma, the inflation-unemployment trade-off, as this is shown in orthodox Phillips curve analysis. Assuming the adaptive expectations procedure the Phillips curve shifts gradually in the course of time, giving an "expectations-augmented Phillips curve". With the aid of a very simple and illustrative model in Chapter 5 an extensive description of the advanced rational-expectations theory is put forward, and the radical implications of this theory for the effectiveness of monetary policy are indicated.[1] The model is amplified and elucidated in the appendix. On the basis of recent literature a critical evaluation of the rational-expectations hypothesis is presented in Chapter 6. Finally in Chapter 7, some recommendations are made to mitigate the destabilizing impact of inflation expectations on the ultimate course of the economic process.

We should like to point out that in this study the analysis concerns the implications of the expectations structure for monetary policy in a closed economy. It is quite clear that such a supposition may be justified for a country like the United States, where the economy is of a rather closed character. However in a country like the Netherlands with a clearly open economy the influence of international economic relations will undoubtedly be substantial, so an extension of the expectations theory to include an open economy would, on the one hand, make the analysis more realistic, but on the other hand it would become more complicated (Mathieson 1977, Duck and Zis, 1979).

1. It must be noticed that in the literature the rational-expectations hypothesis is also applied to formulating expected interest rates and foreign exchange rate expectations. See Dornbusch (1976), Frenkel (1977), Fama (1975).

2. Theoretical foundations of monetary policy: monetarists versus non-monetarists[1]

2.1. Introduction

After the renaissance in monetary theory in the fifties the theoretical foundations of monetary policy were greatly emphasized in economic literature from the mid-sixties. This development is closely related to the fact that the postwar macroeconomic stabilization policy based on Keynesian analysis has not been successful in curbing the inflationary process effectively in recent decades. Also important in this context are the results of empirical studies by Friedman, Meiselman and others which supported the monetarist view that there exists a strong and reasonably stable correlation between changes in the money supply and changes in the amount of national income.

As we know, since the thirties discussions regarding economic stabilization policy are characterized by the idea that monetary policy is relatively ineffective in stabilizing economic development. Since then the proposition that "money doesn't matter" has been supported by many economists in the Keynesian camp, although in recent years the debate has concentrated on the issue "money matters" versus "money only matters". Keynes's doctrine, which focused on aggregate demand management, has had a substantial influence on the theoretical literature and on practical economic policy in the postwar period. Adherents of the Keynesian orthodoxy assume that the

1. This chapter is largely based on the discussion paper presented at the SUERF Colloquium on "New approaches in monetary policy" at Wiesbaden in September 1977. This paper is also published in the proceedings of the colloquium (Sijben 1979).

private sector is inherently unstable and that the need for governmental intervention with a macroeconomic stabilization policy using fiscal measures to mitigate the fluctuations in economic activity is apparent. Monetary policy, measured by changes in the money supply, manifests itself by changes in the rates of interest. Furthermore, this rate of interest, as a cost of capital, is the central variable which links the monetary and the real sector of the economy via investment and consumption expenditures. Keynesians attribute the slight effectiveness of monetary policy to a strong interest-elasticity of the demand for money on the one hand and to a weak interest-elasticity of aggregate expenditures on the other hand. The reason why Keynesians give more attention to fiscal policy in stabilizing economic activity arises from the fact that governmental expenditures and taxes have a more direct and more rapid impact on total demand than monetary-political measures. They hold the view that a decrease in taxes and an increase in governmental expenditures, given the multiplier and accelerator processes, will stimulate the demand for goods and services as well as production and employment. The use of monetary policy in economic stabilization is associated in the Keynesian model with many uncertainties because such policies do not have such a strong and direct relation with the different components of a macroeconomic aggregate demand as fiscal policy. In the Keynesian model full employment policy is in essence based on fiscal policy and the accommodating monetary phenomena. This means that in the Keynesian income-expenditure model the money supply is continuously adjusted to the needs of economic activity and causality proceeds from the real side of the economic process to the monetary side (accommodating monetary policy). According to the earlier view of the "banking principle" the monetary authorities will always supply the amount of money dictated by the development of the real variables in the economy.

After the domination by the Keynesian proponents, or non-monetarists, for a quarter of a century, during the last decade a controversy has arisen between monetarists and Keynesians concerning macroeconomic stabilization policy. The central question was put forward whether untimely and unjustifiable monetary and fiscal measures are the dominant source of fluctuations in economic activity. Subsequently this controversy strongly influenced the development of macroeconomic theory and especially practical monetary policy during the seventies. In the United States during the fifties a revolutionary monetary theory was formulated by Milton Friedman at the University of Chicago and further developed by Brunner and Meltzer and economists of the Federal Reserve Bank of St. Louis, who pointed to some deficiencies in the orthodox Keynesian theory. Modern monetary theoretical views are based on the orthodox quantity theory which has belonged for centuries among the accepted paradigms of the economics profession. Initially in monetary literature this new development was indicated as the Chicago school of thought, but in the course of time the name *monetarism* became current. Samuelson defines the term as follows: "Monetarism is the belief that the primary determinant of the state of macro-economic aggregate demand – whether there will be unemployment – whether there will be inflation – is money, M_1 or M_2, and more specifically, perhaps, its various rates of change" (1969, p. 7). Modigliani however holds the view that the distinction between monetarists and non-monetarists has become less important in an analytical sense, but rather the question whether there still exists a need for a macroeconomic stabilization policy must be considered. The changed view in the Keynesian camp about the role of money in macroeconomics appears from the following quotation: "In reality the distinguishing feature of the monetarist school and the real issues of disagreement with monetarists is not monetarism, but the role that should probably be assigned to stabilization policies" (Modigliani 1977, p. 1). This view is closely connected with the central question in this study, namely, whether there is still any room left for an active monetary policy as a part of macroeconomic stabilization policy in an economic world faced with uncertainty and imperfect information and in which inflationary expectations are playing a dominant role in the economic processes. This actual problem will be analysed in detail later in this study.

Needless to say, a precise analysis of and a clear insight into the complicated transmission process of the monetary impulse are necessary for an effective formulation of monetary policy. The transmission process concerns the question of how money has an impact on economic activity, in other words it describes the mechanism by which monetary actions influence the ultimate goals of macroeconomic policy. Next it is essential to have an insight into the money supply process and to analyse which monetary aggregates should be chosen to judge whether the thrust of monetary actions is neutral, expansive, or contractive with respect to the ultimate targets in the real sector, like employment, production and prices. This last indicator problem is critically dependent, as will further be explained, on the assumed transmission process between the financial and the real sector of the economy. Finally the question arises whether the monetary authorities must follow a money supply rule or a more discretionary policy. This concerns the problem whether a target for money supply growth must be fixed and publicly announced or whether money supply growth must be accommodated to keep pace with economic activity.

The four subjects of the theory of monetary policy mentioned above, i.e., the transmission mechanism, the money supply process, the indicator problem, and monetary targets as alternatives to discretion in the conduct of monetary policy, will be analysed in the following sections.

2.2. The transmission process of monetary impulses

Studying the monetary theoretical literature of the postwar period, it is notable that the speculative component of money demand, introduced by Keynes, stimulated Tobin to develop monetary theory more fully (Tobin 1958). Tobin has explicitly taken account of risk and uncertainty variables in the portfolio composition of the economic subjects (money versus bonds). He pointed out clearly that an individual risk-averting investor, unlike in the Keynesian liquidity-preference theory, will put in his portfolio money and bonds at the same time. Tobin and other economists of Yale University extended the orthodox

Keynesian money-bond model. In the standard Keynesian money-bond model the substitution among wealth-assets is substantially restricted and the interest rate, as a cost-of-capital channel, is the central transmission variable between the monetary and real sector of the economy. Wealth effects are omitted in this analysis. The ultimate impact of an initial nominal demand-pull on the real sector is crucially dependent on the numerical values of the interest-elasticity of the demand for money and of the interest-elasticity of the aggregate expenditures (slopes of the IS–LM curves). In the portfolio analysis it is assumed that individuals, having regard to their wealth position, first of all have to decide what amount of current income they want to save (wealth accumulation), and then have to take a decision with regard to the composition of the portfolio (wealth composition).

In the portfolio-theory it is supposed that in the modern financially highly-developed economies the investor can choose from a spectrum of not totally substitutable assets (real and financial), of which some have a partly monetary character (savings and time deposits). The distinction between different wealth-assets means that not only *one* yield has to be determined as in the standard Keynesian IS–LM model (the bond yield), but a whole spectrum of yields. The portfolio-balance theory has brought about a synthesis, as it were, between the traditional Keynesian approach to the demand for money (money versus bonds) and the views of the former Cambridge School (money versus capital goods), which considered an investment in physical capital goods the only alternative for the holding of real cash balances (Tobin 1961).

In addition to this neo-Keynesian view in monetary theory, Friedman began a monetary counter-revolution by his reformulation of the classical quantity theory and, like Tobin and others, focused on the function of money as an asset (Friedman 1969a). Because money is held as a wealth-asset, the demand for money has to be analysed as a part of a general theory of holding assets. Summarizing we can conclude that in the postwar period neo-Keynesians as well as monetarists have emphasized the important function of money as an asset in their theoretical explanations of its influence on the outcome of the real economic process.

Although both schools of thought have one principal common feature the distinction between the two approaches is expressed in the nature and description of the transmission process through which the monetary impulse ultimately influences economic activity. The description of the transmission mechanism in this section is based on the relative-price theoretical approach developed by Brunner and Meltzer. Friedman, and the monetarists of the Federal Reserve Bank of St. Louis, make use of reduced-form equations in their analyses so no explicit attention is given to the transmission process of monetary impulses. These authors made many empirical studies in the sixties trying to quantify the impact of changes in the money supply and of changes in governmental expenditures on the amount of national income and on the course of economic activity over the business cycle (Andersen and Jordan 1968b). These investigations were dubbed a "black box" by non-monetarists because they were estimations of a reduced model which was not further detailed. And so the linking of variables between the monetary and real sector of the economy remains a mystery. Furthermore it can be noticed that it is less important to know the influence of monetary and fiscal impulses on the amount of national income than the influence on the price and quantity components of national income. Non-monetarists have always preferred relative detailed disaggregated models because they were interested in the impact of impulses on the different aggregative variables. Brunner and Meltzer in particular accepted the challenge of the non-monetarists and laid the theoretical foundations of the monetarist views by making use of the neoclassical relative-price mechanism and the portfolio-balance theory mentioned above.

The ideas of Brunner and Meltzer, who are henceforth referred to as monetarists, with regard to the transmission mechanism present analogies with the neo-Keynesian transmission process based on the supply price of capital, although the assets in the portfolio are enlarged with durable consumer goods and even with the non-material human capital. Opposing the non-monetarists they assume that the private sector is characterized by stable behavioural relationships and that fluctuations in economic activity result from interventions by the government. This means that changes in relative prices or yields of the different financial and physical assets (money, time and savings deposits, bonds, shares, capital goods, and so on) will absorb exogenous shocks and thereby cause the economic system to converge to a new equilibrium situation. The monetarist transmission process is characterized by substitution processes, put in operation by relative prices and by adjustments of wealth of the economic subjects (wealth effects). Brunner and Meltzer do not emphasize strongly the significance of flow variables as do Friedman and the Keynesians but they concentrate especially on the working of the relative-price mechanism and on the stock variables. The portfolios of the individuals consist of money and financial and real assets. The substitution processes concern the mutual substitution between the different assets, between existing assets and newly-produced units, and finally between the purchase of a physical asset and obtaining the services of the asset concerned. The central idea continually emphasized is that an excess supply of any one asset will be directed to that asset with which it has the best substitution relation. After an initial disturbance has occurred the equilibrium in the portfolio will be restored only when an adequate adjustment of relative prices and yields has taken place so that demand and supply of each wealth component are equal. The portfolio decisions of the economic agents give an explanation of the link between the financial and the real sector of the economy, because total wealth consists of real as well as financial assets (Brunner 1971; Brunner and Meltzer 1972).

Previous to the description of the operation of the transmission process it is of essential importance to give some attention to the credit market mechanism of the monetarist model. The credit market also comes into the picture in the money supply process in Section 2.3. The monetarists especially have criticized the orthodox Keynesian doctrine as presented in the postwar economic literature (IS–LM models). In these two-asset models it is supposed that on the one side money and government bonds are imperfect substitutes and on the other side that bonds and physical capital goods are perfect substitutes in the portfolios of the individuals. In this way bonds and real capital goods are considered by individuals as one and the same asset. As a result of this supposition an excess demand for bonds always involves an equal excess supply of money and vice versa. This means that the bond market (credit market) is just the reverse of the money market and, according to Walras' Law, can be eliminated. Therefore it is impossible to analyse methods of financing a budget deficit by a bond issue because the interest rate which is determined by the money market will not be influenced by the total financial transaction. To avoid this, the monetarists explicitly include in their theoretical analysis the operation of the credit market as well as the money market. In this context on balance four markets result, i.e., the market for current production (which determines the price of current production and the production level), the credit market, the money market, and the market for existing capital goods. Furthermore, according to Walras' Law the market for existing capital goods is incorporated into the Walrasian money market so that essentially three markets emerge. It is only the credit market which spreads the government securities over banks and the public and gives individuals the possibility of accomplishing a reallocation of the portfolio. Besides in this market the banks appear as suppliers of credit (buyers of private financial assets) and the public as demanders of credit (sellers of private financial assets). This interaction between banks and the private sector in the credit market determines the rate of interest on financial assets. Contrastingly, in this credit market approach, the money market determines the price at which the economic agents are prepared to include the existing stock of capital goods in their portfolios. This is the supply price of capital which is an important link in the following transmission process (Kuné 1976, p. 481; Nieuwenburg 1977).

The rather complicated monetarist process through which monetary impulses act upon the real variables is as follows: when the central banks pursue an expansive monetary policy by purchasing short-term government securities from the private sector the portfolio balance of the economic agents *will be disturbed*, for this central bank action initially will involve an excess supply of real cash balances which the individuals will want to eliminate by asking for an interest-bearing close substitute. As far as the substitution is directed to bonds an excess demand for bonds and an increase of the price of these financial assets will result. In consequence the bond yield, in relation to the yields of other competitive financial assets in the portfolio, such as shares, declines. According to the mutual substitution hypothesis a further portfolio adjustment comes about and the demand for shares will increase. An increase in the price of shares means a rise in the price of existing capital goods above the price of newly produced units. This price difference gives an incentive to increase investment activity and leads to an expansion of the production of capital goods. This investment impulse gives rise to an increase in economic activity through the operation of the traditional multiplier and accelerator processes. The economic agents then have substituted newly produced capital goods for existing capital goods. This mechanism of the supply price of capital, which is also the essential channel in the neo-Keynesian transmission process, is clearly stated by Brunner as follows.

> Die Neuproduktion von Realkapital ist ein enges Substitut zum vorhandenen Realkapital. Steigende Preise für Vermögensobjekte induzieren auf diese Weise eine Substitution von vorhandenem Realkapital durch neues Kapital. Fölglich nehmen die Investitionsausgaben mit dem Konsumausgaben zu (Brunner 1970, p. 10).

In this quotation it is clearly pointed out that a distinction must be made between the market for existing capital goods and the goods market (current production). In the first market the capital goods available in the period concerned are traded, while in the second market the demands for newly produced capital goods (investment demand) together with the consumption demand are under consideration. This means that two prices for real capital goods result: one for the capital goods still existing and one for the capital goods produced in the period concerned. In the macroeconomic explanations the latter price is equal to the price of consumption goods as part of current production.

As has already been noted the monetarists use a broad wealth conception and include durable consumer goods and even human capital. This involves a situation in which changes in the rate of interest and yields in the financial sector not only result in changes in the demand for investment goods but also in a change in durable consumer goods and in human capital (education and so on). Further the monetarists assume that there exists a lag between the development of prices of goods and services produced by the capital goods and the price development of physical capital. This also gives rise to a substitution process between the demand for physical capital goods themselves and the demand for the goods and services produced by the assets concerned (renting instead of building a house), whereby economic activity will likewise be stimulated.

The neoclassical theory of the relative-price approach to monetary analysis emphasizes that the monetary impulse ultimately manifests itself in a demand expansion on all markets as a consequence of many substitution processes within the portfolio of the economic subjects.

Finally the monetarists stress the operation of the wealth effect, which comes about in two ways. First of all a decline in the rate of interest induced by the expansive monetary impulse results in an increase in the value of the existing assets (indirect wealth effect). Monetarists assume that wealth is an important determinant of consumption expenditures, so that these expenditures will be adjusted in the same direction as wealth. Summarizing this it appears that macroeconomic aggregate demand will be influenced in two ways: on the one side by the substitution processes described above and on the other side by the wealth effects induced by the fall in the rate of interest. The operation of the substitution effect as well as of the wealth effect with regard to aggregate demand proceeds in the same direction. Secondly it is possible that the monetary impulse as such involves a change in the net wealth position of the private sector (direct wealth effect). There are many controversies in monetary literature concerning the question of assets comprising the total wealth of the private sector, but in any case it can be said that as far as the monetary impulse is related to outside money there will be a change in the net wealth position of the private sector and so in expenditures in the same direction.[2] In this context the question arises as to whether interest-bearing government bonds owned by individuals might also be considered a net wealth component. Monetarists take the line that financing the budget deficit with the aid of bonds does contribute to an increase in net wealth of the private sector. This view is strongly based on the essential supposition that individuals do not capitalize the future tax obligations on behalf of interest and redemption. When the greater part of future tax obligations is capitalized an accordingly weaker wealth effect will arise and consequently deficit financing through bonds will have a weaker impact on total expenditures in the economy (Sijben 1977, pp. 170–172).

Summarizing, we may conclude that the monetarists, and especially Brunner and Meltzer, have refuted the criticisms of the non-monetarists with regard to the idea of the "black box" in the recent past by giving a clear analysis of processes through which monetary impulses act upon economic activity. This action takes place through a very complicated portfolio adjustment process, whereby the relative yields of the different assets, the wealth effects and the mutual substitution relations among these assets perform a strategic role.

2.3. The money supply process

In orthodox Keynesian theory where the demand function for money (liquidity preference theory) is emphasized the supply of money is entered as an exogenous variable. The assumption of an autonomous money supply implies that the central bank can always apply the available instruments of monetary policy in such a way that the desired amount of money will be achieved. This view is based on the essential mechanics of the money creation process, indicated in the literature as the theory of the

2. Outside money is a completely liquid financial asset of the monetary authority with no debt from the public to the issuer.

mechanical money multiplier. The theory points out that there exists a simple and, especially, a mechanical relation between the money supply and the completely liquid assets (base money) created by the central bank. Such a conclusion is an abstraction of the actual money supply process, for in this way no attention is given to the fact that the money supply process is essentially the result of a continuous interaction between the monetary behaviour of the banking system (including the "para-monetary" financial institutions), the government and the public with regard to the composition of their portfolios.

In contrast monetarists (Friedman, Schwartz, Cagan, and later Brunner and Meltzer) assume that the money supply is also determined by endogenous factors (Friedman and Schwartz 1963; Cagan 1965; Brunner 1961; Korteweg 1971). This means that the credit supply of the commercial banking system based on the profit maximization principle and portfolio behaviour is crucially dependent on the yields of the different financial assets. In this way the money supply is determined in part endogenously and will be the result of an interaction among the activities of the central bank, the treasury, the commercial banks and the private sector with regard to the composition of their portfolios. In this context we may refer to the activities of commercial banks concerning the excess reserve ratio, actions of individuals with regard to their preference for currency relative to demand and time deposits, and so on. By making use of the instruments of monetary policy the central bank disturbs the equilibrium of portfolios both for commercial banks and for the public, through which disturbance portfolio adjustment processes will arise changing the money supply. Brunner expresses this view in the following way: "This program suggests that the public and banks interact in the determination of bank credit, interest rates and the money stock, in response to the behavior of monetary authorities" (1968, p. 24).

On the basis of many theoretical and empirical studies the monetarists come to the conclusion that the monetary authorities can control the movements in the money stock and that the money supply is a good indicator of the thrust of central bank actions on the ultimate targets in the real sector of the economy (see Section 2.4). When we hold the view that the money supply is a dominant factor accounting for variations in the ultimate targets (output, employment and prices), then it is quite obvious that the relations among the instruments of monetary policy and the money stock should be analysed. Monetarists assume with regard to the money supply mechanism that the monetary base is a suitable guide for monetary policy because the amount of this variable can be controlled by the central bank. Changes in the monetary base not proceeding from the interventions of the central bank can be set aside as being insignificant quantitatively.

In the money supply process of the monetarists the money stock is presented as the product of a money multiplier and the monetary base. This money multiplier summarizes as it were all the economic and institutional factors which constitute a link between changes in the monetary base, some monetary aggregates like the money stock (narrowly or broadly defined), and bank credit. The money supply process according to the monetary-base approach can be described along the following simple lines.[3] The monetary base (B) is money supplied by the central bank and which the commercial banks are required to hold as a cash reserve (R) against their deposit liabilities and which is desired as currency (C) by the non-bank public. This completely liquid financial asset, issued by the monetary authority, is usually indicated by neo-quantity theorists as high-powered money. This is expressed in algebraic terms in the following way:

$$B = R + C \tag{1}$$

When the central bank determines a cash-reserve requirement (r_d and r_t) for commercial banks to hold against their demand deposits (D) and time deposits (T), whereby $r_d > r_t$, and as far as the banking system desires to hold excess reserves (E), the following equation results:

3. For a clear and detailed money supply analysis see Burger (1972), Korteweg (1971, pp. 9–28), and Goodhart (1975).

$$R = r_d D + r_t T + E \tag{2}$$

From equation (2) the supply of demand deposits emerges:

$$D = \frac{R - r_t T - E}{r_d} \tag{3}$$

Next adding up the currency in the hands of the non-bank public the total money supply (M) can be derived as follows:

$$M = C + \frac{R - r_t T - E}{r_d} \tag{4}$$

From equation (4) we come to the tentative conclusion that the money supply is determined by six factors of which three are dependent on the behaviour of monetary authorities (R, r_d and r_t), two are determined by the non-bank public (C and T), and one is dependent on the monetary behaviour of the commercial banking system (E). The excess reserves (E), defined as the difference between the total bank reserves and the required reserves, are held by the commercial banking system for the following reasons: on the one hand there is a desire to hold excess reserves to bear up against the future risk of deposit loss (precautionary motive); and on the other hand, the banks want to keep open the possibility of investing these reserves in a more profitable way in due time (speculative motive). This entails in essence a trade-off between a good liquidity position and high profitability for the banks. This choice does not appear in the traditional mechanical money supply theory where it is supposed that the banks always stay "fully loaned up".

Next, assuming that the public desires a ratio (c) of currency to private demand deposits and a ratio (t) of interest-bearing time deposits to demand deposits and assuming that the commercial banking system desires a ratio (e) of excess reserves to demand deposits, equation (1) can be reformulated as follows:

$$B = (r_d + r_t t + e + c)D \tag{1'}$$

The relation between the monetary base and demand deposits can now be rendered as

$$D = \frac{1}{r_d + r_t t + e + c} B \tag{5}$$

Finally, since the money supply is the sum of demand deposits and currency, the relation of the money supply to the monetary base is simply

$$M = \frac{1+c}{r_d + r_t t + e + c} B \tag{6}$$

The term $(1+c)/(r_d + r_t t + e + c)$ can be called the money supply multiplier and represents the number of times by which the money supply (M) exceeds the volume of base money (B). The money supply function (6) shows that the money stock in the economy is determined by the following variables:

1. The volume of base money supplied by the monetary authority (B);
2. The reserve requirement percentage against demand deposits (r_d) and against time deposits (r_t), set by the central bank;
3. The desired currency ratio (c) determined by the non-bank public;
4. The desired time deposit ratio (t) also determined by the non-bank public;
5. Finally, the desired excess reserve ratio (e) determined by the commercial banking system.

Assuming that the three factors, c, t and e, which represent the portfolio behaviour of banks and the public, are fixed ratios, it can be said that the central bank can straightforwardly control the size of the money supply by controlling the volume of base money (B) and the cash reserve requirements (r_d and r_t). In practice, however, these desired ratios are not constant but are crucially dependent on the yields of the different wealth assets, the discount rate set by the central bank, and the level of economic activity. If we consider, for example, a change in the desired time deposit ratio (t) of the public the following process will evolve. An increase in the rate of interest paid on time deposits may give rise to a substitution process, because people want to hold fewer demand deposits, resulting in an increase in the desired time deposit ratio (t). These financial transactions will free reserves ($r_t < r_d$) and the excess reserves of the banks are increased which can then be used to supply additional bank credit to adjust the excess reserves to the desired level. As can be deduced from equation (6) the numerical value of the money multiplier decreases which means that on balance the same volume of base money now represents a lesser amount of money than it would otherwise.

The same reasoning can be followed when it is desirable for the commercial banking system to reduce the excess reserve ratio (e), due to a lower discount rate and or to an increase in the market-determined interest rate, or when the public wants to reduce the desired currency ratio (c), because of a preference for making payments by cheque accounts. In both cases a portfolio adjustment process will take place by which the magnitude of the money supply multiplier increases and the supply of bank credit and the money supply is extended. Under certain circumstances it may even occur that when an extension of bank credit is very attractive the commercial banks may accept net borrowed reserves (borrowed reserves at the central bank exceed excess reserves).[4]

From this very simple money supply analysis we may conclude that changes in the magnitude of the money multiplier are essentially reflections of the portfolio decisions made by the commercial banks, the treasury and the public. This monetary behaviour is dependent on the development of economic activity, the market interest rates and future expectations. Changes in base money incorporate monetary policy actions of the central bank (discount and open-market policy and reserve requirement changes). These changes in base money may influence interest rates which further may give rise to a change in the numerical value of the money multiplier. The wealth-theoretical approach in the money supply process has led to the fundamental view that the commercial banking system, like the

---

4. For empirical studies with regard to the money supply process see Rasche (1972) and Neldner (1977, pp. 2–5).

public, must be considered economically calculating categories instead of technically-mechanically-acting economic agents. The amount of base money and the realized required-reserve percentage are not exclusively determined by the instruments of monetary policy but also by the rational portfolio decisions of the banking system and the public. In this way the simple money supply theory described above links up well with the reformulation of the quantity theory as a wealth-theoretical explanation of the demand for money (Korteweg 1971, p. 208). Although it appears from our analysis that the money stock is also determined by endogenous factors, expressed by variations in the magnitude of the money supply multiplier, monetarists still hold the view that on balance the money supply is an exogenous, controllable, economic variable. Empirical evidence supports the view that movements in base money dominate the movements in the total money supply (Rasche 1972, p. 11; Jordan 1969).

2.4. Selecting an indicator of monetary policy

The explanations concerning the transmission processes and the concomitant question of formulating an efficient monetary policy strategy have divided theorists and practitioners since the end of the sixties into two camps: the monetarists and the non-monetarists, or Keynesians. At that time monetary authorities had not drawn up an explicit monetary policy framework and no targets were detailed with regard to monetary variables. Monetary policy strategy involves a closed circle of interconnections in the model between the instruments of monetary policy and some intermediate variables on the one hand and between these intermediate variables and the ultimate objectives in the real sector (production, employment, and so on) on the other hand.

Because monetary policy measures operate upon economic activity with substantial but variable, time lags, monetary authorities cannot observe an immediate impact of their actions on the ultimate strategic objectives in the real sector. The monetary policy decision process can be divided into two phases. First of all the monetary authorities have to decide upon the ultimate objectives for monetary policy – with the choice of these objectives policy dilemmas, such as the conflicting goals of full employment and price stability, may arise. Second, policymakers must decide how to manipulate the different policy instruments to achieve the ultimate objectives in the real sector. In practice and also in theory (for monetarists and non-monetarists), there is almost no disagreement with regard to the fixation of ultimate targets in terms of real production, employment and prices. However there are many controversies concerning the second question, referring to the link between the instruments of monetary policy and the ultimate policy targets.

It is quite obvious that monetary policy implementation would be much easier if there were complete information about the accurate operation of the monetary transmission process and so about the interrelations between policy instruments and financial and real variables. In such a case monetary policy would merely involve manipulating the instruments in a way that would result in known and desired effects on the levels and rates of change of the ultimate policy targets. However because in practice there is a lack of complete information about the complicated transmission processes, whereby the ultimate effects of monetary policy actions are spread throughout the period concerned, the following pragmatic procedure has come to the fore. Makers of monetary policy introduce certain intermediate variables which can give the necessary information in implementing monetary policy. From a pragmatic point of view the monetary policy decision process is divided into a number of segments and policymakers have introduced the indicator-operational target approach to improve the implementation of monetary policy (Burger 1971). This approach which focuses on operational targets and indicators can be rendered schematically as follows:

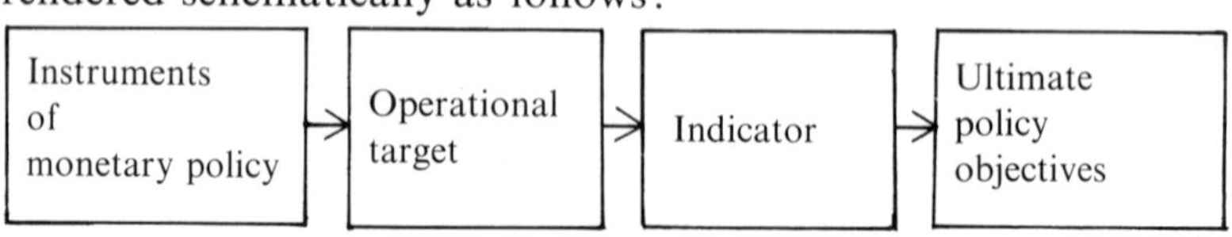

In the first place it is desirable to give a clear definition of the two conceptions, the *indicator* and the *operational target*, and to investigate which financial variables are suitable. The question of the intermediate targets has arisen frequently in the discussions in monetary theoretical literature in the last few years and has rekindled the controversy between monetarists and non-monetarists (Board of Governors of the Federal Reserve System 1971; Federal Reserve Bank of New York 1974). A first problem arises with regard to the interpretation of the effect of monetary policy measures on the ultimate policy targets in the real sector. Then the question arises as to which indicator(s) may be used to judge whether the current monetary actions exert a neutral, an expansive, or a contractive influence on the ultimate targets. This judging process cannot occur when one is dealing with economic variables like the unemployment rate or the rate of inflation because current changes in these variables may well be the result of monetary actions in previous periods. The answer to the foregoing question is closely related to the individual interpretation of the operation of the transmission process as the link through which monetary policy affects economic activity. Such an indicator is intended to give information about the current impact of monetary impulses on the course of the ultimate policy targets. The indicator must be an adequate representation of the ultimate targets and turns up as the last link in the chain in the transmission process. In principle every monetary variable may be suitable, provided that the following requirements are met. First of all a change in the magnitude of the indicator should have a strong predictable impact on the fixed policy objectives in the real sector of the economy. Next, reliable information with regard to the magnitude of the indicator must be readily available to the monetary authorities. Finally, the makers of monetary policy should be able to control this indicator accurately so that a change in its magnitude can be interpreted as the result of their own monetary actions. Non-monetarists prefer in this context a price target (a market interest rate), whereas the monetarists focus on a quantity target (a monetary aggregate). This question will be considered in more detail further on in this section.

A second problem in formulating a monetary policy strategy, linked with the controllability of the indicator, arises because there is no direct and unambiguous relation among the instruments of monetary policy and the chosen indicator, for when an instrument of monetary policy is activated it may be possible that during the operation other economic factors influence the indicator so that it will give rise to misleading information about the impact of monetary actions. Consequently this could easily result in a wrong judgement of current monetary policy. Also in this context makers of monetary policy prefer a pragmatic procedure by introducing so-called operational targets, which can improve the implementation of monetary policy. This operational target is a monetary variable which in its turn acts as a direction indicator for the indicator chosen initially. It is a variable which in principle should be controlled by the central bank through its day-to-day operations in the money market. The operational target can be considered as the "monetary fuel" supplied by the monetary authorities, while the indicator gives the central bank a reading as to how far this fuel is converted to "monetary energy" to drive the economic activity. The operational target should satisfy the following three criteria (Burger 1971, p. 22; Heremans *et al.* 1975; Zijlstra 1979, p. 15). It is of essential importance that the central bank be able to measure accurately the magnitude of this target over very short periods of time, preferably from day to day. In this way makers of monetary policy can ascertain whether or not the influence of their monetary actions is going in the right direction, and so achieving the desired effect on the ultimate policy targets. Next the central bank should be able to control the operational target by manipulating monetary policy instruments. Finally it is necessary that changes in the magnitude of the operational target dominate changes in the magnitude of the chosen indicator. The choice of the operational target is also crucially dependent on the interpretation of the transmission process. In this context non-monetarists prefer to use money-market conditions (short-term interest rates, free reserves of commercial banks, and so on), whereas monetarists rather emphasize the use of the monetary base as the operational target because this variable can be controlled very well by the central bank and has a good predictable relation with a number of monetary aggregates acting as indicators.

Starting from the monetary policy decision described above it is desirable to trace which monetary variables can be used as indicators and as operational targets. It should be noted in advance that it is not possible to use as an indicator a price target and a quantity target simultaneously. If the central bank attempted to control the interest rate the money stock would fluctuate violently. Conversely if the money supply were controlled erratic fluctuations of the rate of interest would result. Further it can be noticed that there is no need for an operational target when the monetary authorities control the indicator directly. In this context we can think of a direct control of the absolute amount of bank credit to the private sector or of fixing a certain rate of growth of bank credit.

As has already been mentioned, monetarists have always given the money supply strong preference over the rate of interest as an indicator of monetary policy. This view is pronounced by Brunner,

> Therefore, the monetarist thesis puts forth the proposition that actions of the Federal Reserve are transmitted to economic activity via the resulting movements in the monetary base and money supply, which initiate the adjustments in relative prices of assets, liabilities and the production of new assets (Brunner 1968, p. 20).

In Keynesian macroeconomics (IS–LM analysis) however, changes in the money supply influence the pace of economic activity mainly by changes in the long-term interest rate as a cost-of-capital channel (indicator). The operational target is concentrated on those variables which represent banking and money market conditions. This view is strongly based on orthodox Keynesianism whereby changes in interest rates influence investment expenditures and consequently, via the operation of the multiplier and accelerator mechanism, the course of economic activity.

The use of the long-term market rate of interest as an indicator of monetary policy has been discussed in monetary literature since the mid-sixties. Criticism, especially expressed by monetarists, is focused on an identification problem. This relates to the difficulty of making a distinction between changes in interest rates resulting from demand impulses (real sector) and changes which are generated by monetary policy actions (monetary sector). Consequently the signals from these interest rates may easily result in a misleading judgement of the current monetary situation. In these circumstances monetary authorities might be tempted to take actions which then give rise to a pro-cyclical monetary policy. In this context monetarists emphasize the relation which exists between an expansive monetary policy and a rising instead of a falling rate of interest (the Gibson paradox). A first reasoning for this phenomenon arises from the interactions between the money, the product, and the credit markets, which play an essential part in the monetarist transmission process (see Section 2.2). The monetarists point out that when the expansive monetary impulse influences economic activity through the substitution and wealth adjustment processes, feedback effects will arise from the real sector increasing the demand for bank credit. This means that the initial fall in the interest rate (Keynesian liquidity effect) will be more than compensated for by a rise in the interest rate as a consequence of a higher transaction demand for money (income-effect) on the one hand, and the induced increase in the public demand for bank credit on the other hand (credit-market effect). This rise in the rate of interest very well might be interpreted in this context as the result of a restrictive monetary policy, while an expansionary monetary policy was the origin of the interaction process. An analogous reasoning could be followed in the case of an initial contractionary monetary policy. Another explanation for the reasons why changes in the rate of interest and in the money supply often give misleading information about the judgement of the actual monetary situation is linked with the classical Fisher-effect viewpoint. Maintaining a low interest rate in order to stimulate economic activity will necessitate a constant increase in the money supply. However this easy money policy in itself generates an inflationary development and gives rise to inflationary expectations. In the long run these inflationary expectations will influence the nominal rate of interest in a way which was not aimed at by the monetary authorities (Fisher's price-expectations effect). Then a rising rate of interest in an inflationary environment may be an indication for the policy-makers that the expansionary monetary policy did not work. In those circumstances monetary authorities, often under pressure of public opinion, will be apt to speed further the expansionary monetary policy with the only result being the strengthening of the current inflationary process. This means that with inflationary expectations economic agents become progressively more accustomed to the inflation phenomenon and consequently adjust their economic behaviour (see Chapters 4 and 5), so lenders will no longer be subjected to the well-known money illusion and will try to secure themselves with loan contracts by claiming an inflation compensation, expressed in a sufficiently higher nominal rate of interest to compensate for the capital loss on interest and redemption.

From the explanations mentioned above we may conclude, especially with regard to the recent decade, that the reliance on the rate of interest as an indicator of monetary policy is weakened substantially because of the operation of the credit-market effect and the price-expectations effect.[5] Monetarists rather consider a rising rate of interest as an indication that economic activity is increased and point out that makers of monetary policy should be very cautious in using monetary policy to stimulate economic activity. A rising rate of interest, which is the price of credit, must be considered as an expression of an increasing demand for bank credit induced by an economic recovery and not as an expression of a current monetary tightness.

Non-monetarists mostly choose the free reserves with the commercial banks as the operational target. These free reserves are defined as the difference between the current excess and the borrowed reserves at the central bank. In a broader context these free reserves can be viewed as a substitute for a number of

5. For empirical support for these views see Gibson (1970, 1972) and Yohe and Karnosky (1969).

short-term money-market interest rates (treasury bill rate and call-money rate). The choice of free reserves as an operational target is based on the following consideration. According to the theory of the traditional mechanical money and credit multiplier, the commercial banking system will always try to eliminate current excess reserves by adjusting bank credit supply and concomitantly increasing the money supply. In these circumstances the banking system is always "fully loaned up". However in the free reserves conception it is assumed that the banking system is only willing to make credit adjustments insofar as there exists a "net free reserve position" (excess reserves exceed borrowed reserves). Nevertheless it may be wondered whether the reluctance hypothesis, according to which bankers prefer not to borrow from the central bank, is still consistent with their portfolio analysis and profit maximization behaviour. For the higher the yield on assets in the credit market and the lower the discount rate the less reluctant will the bankers be to borrow from the central bank. This means that free reserves do not perform a mechanical function in such a way that a change in these free reserves will always result in a change in the supply of bank credit and in the money supply in the same direction (Nieuwenburg 1973, p. 557). Rather the demand for free reserves by banks is dependent on the sensitivity of the demand for excess reserves and for borrowings with regard to changes in the yield of assets in the credit market and in the discount rate of the central bank. This means that free reserves have to be considered as an endogenous variable which cannot be sufficiently controlled by the central bank.

As previously noted monetarists have chosen quantity targets to perform the function of intermediate targets. Empirical studies have shown that two monetary aggregates, i.e. the monetary base and the money supply, conform best to the requirements of an operational target and of an indicator respectively. Monetarists hold the view that monetary policy is essentially a quantity policy as a result of which the interest rate is determined. The choice of the money supply as an indicator of monetary policy is largely based on empirical studies which prove that there exists a clear association and a good predictable relation between movements in the money supply and movements in economic activity, in production, employment and prices (Keran 1970; Tanner 1972; Board of Governors of the Federal Reserve System 1971; Federal Reserve Bank of New York 1974). It has also been pointed out that the money stock defined in a narrow sense (M_1), currency in circulation and demand deposits, shows a better positive correlation with national income than does the money stock in a broad sense ($M_2 = M_1$ plus time and savings deposits at commercial banks). This results from the fact that the interest sensitivity of the money and credit multipliers with regard to the money stock in a broad sense (M_2) is higher, which involves the situation in which the magnitude of these multipliers is less stable and more sensitive to induced interest changes from the real sector.

With regard to the operational target it is imperative that this variable be accurately controlled by the central bank (Andersen and Jordan 1968a; Andersen 1975). As was pointed out in Section 2.3, in the wealth-theoretical approach of the money supply process, the money stock is the product of a money multiplier and the monetary base, both of which are determined by the portfolio behaviour of the central bank, the commercial banking system and the public. It has appeared from empirical studies that the adjusted monetary base is the most important determinant of the money supply (M_1), and that this variable can be controlled very well by the open-market operations of the central bank. The question concerning the controllability of the monetary base and of the money supply is analysed at length in monetary literature. With reference to his theoretical and empirical studies, Korteweg (1974) comes to the tentative conclusion that in the short run the money supply in an open economy, as exists in the Netherlands, is controllable in principle by the open-market operations of the central bank. However it is an important condition in this context that the domestic economy can sufficiently be covered from interest-induced international capital movements. This will be impossible in the long run when the central bank aims at maintaining fixed exchange rates – price target (Burger *et al.* 1969; Meltzer 1971).

The ability of the central bank to control the money supply, especially in the short run, is strongly dependent on forecasting all the variables which cannot be directly controlled. In this context we can first think of questions such as the interest sensitivity of the desired currency ratio, the demand for excess reserves by the banking system, and so on, which determine the magnitude of the money and credit multiplier. However the controllability of the monetary base itself is also of crucial importance, especially, as Korteweg points out, with regard to an open economy, since an external source of base money is built up by the purchase of gold and through foreign currency transactions by the banking system, the treasury and the public. Besides the way of financing the budget deficit also influences the amount of base money. However it is worth noting that a precise coordination of the financial decisions of the government with the central bank policy can solve this control problem. Finally the monetary base can also be built up by the discount facilities and loans of the central bank on behalf of the commercial banking system. Although the central bank fixes the discount rate (a price), the banks make the decision as to the level to which they want to make use of these facilities and loans. In this way also monetary authorities partially lose control of the monetary base. In order to increase the controllability of the monetary base monetary authorities could give consideration to an introduction of rediscount quotas.

The monetary control process according to the monetarist views can be simply represented in the following way. First of all makers of monetary policy should convert the ultimate policy targets from the real sector into an accordingly consistent rate of growth of the money supply. This growth rate, which can be considered an indicator, could be translated into a desired rate of growth for the monetary base, assuming a certain magnitude of the multiplier for the planning period (a month). Eventually it may even include weekly and daily changes in the monetary base. Finally the desired level of the monetary base or changes in this variable should be converted into open-market operations of the central bank.

2.5. Rules versus discretion in monetary policy

The monetarist proposition that movements in the money stock are the most important determinants of movements in economic activity and that the development of the money supply is the most reliable indicator of current monetary actions has raised the question of what are the guidelines for implementing monetary policy. Should monetary policy be implemented in a more discretionary way, like the non-monetarists propose, or should the policymakers publicly announce a certain monetary growth rate? In a discretionary monetary policy the behaviour of the monetary authorities can be described as a reaction function, i.e. a monetary policy rule of conduct with feedback effects from the ultimate policy targets in the real sector ("policy activism" or "fine tuning"). This operating guideline for monetary policy links up strongly with the post-Keynesian model, which assumes that the instruments of economic policy, including monetary policy, should be used in a discretionary way to mitigate fluctuations in economic activity. The second guideline, assuming a preannouncement of a certain monetary growth target, finds more response among the monetarists. They postulate that the economy is inherently stable through the operation of the relative-price mechanism so that there is no need for a discretionary monetary policy (see Chapter 5).

These questions were raised in the thirties by Simons, who said, "In a free enterprise system we obviously need highly definite and stable rules of the game, especially as to money. The monetary rules must be compatible with the reasonably smooth working of the system" (Simons 1936). With reference to his detailed empirical study, Friedman comes to a conclusion which is closely related to Simons's view. Friedman points out that the freedom of action of the monetary authorities should be restricted because the observed economic fluctuations arise from erratic variations in the stock of money. The course of movements in the money stock is a major factor accounting for variations in economic activity over the business cycle

(Friedman and Schwartz 1963). He holds the view that makers of monetary policy pay too much attention to the current economic situation and make too little allowance for the result of their actions in the long run when the economic situation may be quite different. Friedman focuses on the significance of the several variable time lags which determine the ultimate effectiveness of monetary policy. If the monetary authorities want to fight a certain economic phenomenon it may be conceivable that their monetary interventions will produce an effect only at a moment when the initial disturbance is still eliminated by other economic forces. In these circumstances the monetary actions produce a pro-cyclical effect decreasing economic stability rather than increasing it. Based on the existence of a long and variable time lag with regard to the impact of monetary policy and due to his belief in the stabilizing forces of the market mechanism and the stable behavioural relationships in the private sector, Friedman prefers a fixed rate of growth of the money supply, disregarding the current economic situation, over a discretionary monetary policy. He holds the view that the monetary authorities should construct a monetary framework that on the one hand restores a sense of greater stability and confidence in economic performance and on the other hand prevents the situation in which monetary actions become a cause of economic instability. With regard to the magnitude of the monetary growth rate Friedman says, "The precise rate of growth, like the precise monetary total, is less important than the adoption of some stated and known rate" (Friedman 1968).

As is well-known from economic literature, in 1975 monetary authorities in the Federal Republic of Germany, Switzerland, Canada and the United States in principle abandoned the discretionary policy strategy and adopted publicly announced money supply targets. In this context Schlesinger of the Deutsche Bundesbank points out, "The Bundesbank first set and publicly announced a quantitative target for monetary policy – an increase of about 8 per cent in central bank money in the course of 1975 – in December 1974" (Schlesinger 1976, p.

6).[6] Although no other central banks have made similar changes in the strategy of monetary policy there are signs that more are contemplating such a move. In a recent annual report of the Dutch central bank the president Dr. Zijlstra speaks about a monetarist revival and states, "The liquidity supply has become so ample at the moment that maintaining it would bring about a self-supporting source of inflation" and he goes on to say, "It would be a misunderstanding to suppose that a monetary target formulated in terms of a liquidity ratio is something quite different from a policy guide in terms of a desired rate of growth of the money supply" (De Nederlandsche Bank 1976, pp. 20–21).[7]

It is very interesting to consider the importance of the conception of a monetary growth target against the background of two macroeconomic policy objectives, full employment and price stability, which have been given considerable attention in the postwar period and especially within the last decade. As we know from the economic literature the trade-off between inflation and unemployment is usually expressed by the Phillips curve. The original version of this curve includes elements of the Keynesian demand-pull inflation theory as well as of the income or cost-push inflation theory. In view of this curve it is possible to determine what are the social costs in terms of unemployment of certain wishes of policymakers with respect to price stability, and vice versa. It is quite obvious that politicians hold different views about the question of whether inflation or unemployment must be considered as the greater social evil. Politicians supporting the Keynesian doctrine will consider unemployment as the most important enemy of the people while accepting a certain rate of inflation as a less dangerous concomitant phenomenon. However if politicians focus on

6. With regard to the central bank money Schlesinger (1976, p. 12) says: "In the end, admittedly, the movement of central bank money does not differ very greatly from that of M_3".

7. In the annual report of 1978 Dr. Zijlstra speaks of a sound rule of monetary growth, involving a growth in the money supply in accordance with that of real national income (De Nederlandsche Bank 1978, p. 20).

maintaining the real purchasing power of money, then a loss of employment has to be accepted as a necessary but politically unacceptable remedy.

In the next chapters the question regarding rules versus discretion in monetary policy will be analysed in detail with regard to two expectations procedures concerning the building up of inflationary expectations by the economic agents. As was already noticed in the first chapter of this study, expectations with regard to economic variables play a significant role in the ultimate course of the economic process. These expectations, and particularly the inflationary expectations, will undoubtedly have a meaning in solving the problem about "policy activism" versus "monetary targets" and also in answering the question as to how far monetary policy still has a meaning in macro-economic stabilization policy.

3. Expectations in retrospect

Since the origins of the economic sciences people's expectations regarding the future values of some crucial economic variables have always drawn a great deal of interest. This especially results when in economic models the actual expectations of market participants with regard to the values of some endogenous variables influence the behaviour equations in a critical way. In particular in the field of monetary economics, expectations theory, most of all with regard to inflation expectations, has been strongly emphasized in recent years. This is connected with the fact that the expected rate of inflation plays an essential role in the determination of some central macroeconomic variables. So the expected rate of inflation is a strategic factor in the explanation of the development of employment and interest rates. Both in macroeconomic theory and in empirical research there is a lack of directly observable data about the expected values of the relevant economic variables, such as the rate of inflation. Usually, therefore, the scientist is forced to make use of data which are approximations of the variables involved. The procedure mostly used in this context is to suppose that expectations about a certain economic variable are linearly related to the actual historical value of the variable concerned (adaptive expectations hypothesis).

The interest in the significance of expectations in an uncertain world characterized by a lack of information dates from the distant past and can be found in the philosophical publications of Locke in 1689. However, Marshall and Keynes were the first authors who explicitly took account of and introduced expectations in economic sciences. Marshall assumed that expectations with regard to profits and to changes in the purchasing power of money (inflation) are important in describing the impact of changes in the money supply on the rate of interest. In this context he remarked:

> The influx of a good deal of bullion into the city is likely to lower the level of discount. When this has been done there is more capital in the hands of speculative investors, who come to the market for goods as buyers, and so raise prices. *Further the influx of bullion will have caused people to expect a rise in prices*, and therefore to be more inclined to borrow for speculative investments . . . causing a rise in the rate of discount (Marshall 1923, p. 256).

In this quotation Marshall points out that an expansion of the money supply will initially result in a lower rate of interest (liquidity effect) and subsequently in an expansion of aggregate demand. He also suggests that the economic agents are so clever and well-informed about the working of the economic process that they anticipate the inflation which will be generated by the monetary expansion and take the appropriate economic decisions.

The significance of a direct relation between the monetary actions of the central bank and the inflation expectations is also put forward by Keynes (1930) in his well-known book *A treatise on money*. This author states with regard to the behaviour of the entrepreneurs:

> Strictly, therefore, we should say that it is the *anticipated* profit or loss which is the mainspring of change and it is by causing *anticipations* of the appropriate kind that the banking system is able to influence the price level. Indeed, it is well-known that one reason for the rapid efficacy of changes in bank rate in modifying the actions of the entrepreneurs is the anticipations to which they give rise. Thus entrepreneurs will sometimes begin to act before the price changes which are the justification of their actions actually occurred (1930, p. 159).

This means that changes in the bank rate perform the function of a signal for the entrepreneurs to change their minds, because they know the impact of these changes on the variables of the economic system. Further on in the same chapter Keynes points to the critical importance of the acquisition and utilization of information about the workings of the economic system in forecasting the expected values of the economic variables. He states:

> All the same, accurate forecasting in these matters is so difficult and requires so much more information than is usually available, that the average behaviour of entrepreneurs in fact is mainly governed by current experience supplemented by such broad generalizations as those relating to the probable consequences of changes in the bank rate, the supply of credit and the state of foreign exchanges. Moreover, actions based on inaccurate anticipations will not long survive experiences of a contrary character, so that the facts will soon override anticipations except where they agree (1930, p. 160).

These two quotations from the *Treatise on money* clearly point out that Keynes considers the economic agents as individuals who take their decisions rationally. Assuming a market exhibiting profit maximization behaviour participants are intensively involved in the acquisition and utilization of information about the behaviour of monetary authorities to make unbiased forecasts of the expected rate of inflation. In this respect Keynes's view links up well with the rational-expectations theory presented by Muth (1961) and explicitly introduced in macroeconomic theory since the early seventies. The rational-expectations theory, which is centred in the recent monetary-theoretical literature, will be more fully analysed in chapters 5 and 6 of this study.

Next to this more rational approach or "strong variant" of the expectations theory (in this study especially with regard to inflation expectations) there also exists a "weak variant" in the relevant economic literature. This latter is characterized by the fact that in forecasting the expected economic variables economic agents only take account of information about the past history of the variable concerned.[1]

Fisher may be indicated as the founder of the adaptive expectations theory because he was the first who explicitly

1. The distinction between a "weak" and a "strong" variant of the expectations hypothesis was introduced in the literature by Fama (1970), who has shifted attention from regressions of interest rates on past inflation rates (Fisher's approach) to the relation between interest rates and the expected rate of inflation (Muth's approach).

introduced a model of building-up inflation expectations. This comes about in his theoretical and empirical expositions about the relation between the nominal and real rate of interest on the one side and the expected rate of inflation on the other side. He was fully aware of the fact that there exists "imperfect foresight" in the real economic world. Although he perceived a relation between the nominal rate of interest and the rate of inflation, it was not his opinion that this relation would result from a conscious adjustment of the money rate of interest to the expected price changes. In this context Fisher remarks:

> It should be noted that insofar as there exists any adjustment of the money rate of interest to the changes in the purchasing power of money, it is for the most part (1) lagged and (2) indirect. The lag, distributed, has been shown to extend over several years. The indirectness of the effect of changed purchasing power comes largely through the intermediate steps which affect business profits and volumes of trade, which in turn affect the demand for loans and the rate of interest. There is very little direct and conscious adjustment through foresight. Where such foresight is conspicuous, as in the final period of German inflation, there is less lag in the effects (Fisher 1930, p. 494; see also Rutledge 1977).

The cautious and general terms of Fisher in this quotation indicate that he does not start from rational individual economic agents, who consciously build up their inflation expectations with the aid of a costly process of acquiring and utilizing information, but that in reality there exists a more or less irrational learning process (error-learning hypothesis). When there is a strong inflationary environment economic agents will become progressively more accustomed to the inflation phenomenon and consequently adjust their economic behaviour so that the lags will be shortened. Contrary to the views of the Cambridge School of Marshall and Keynes, Fisher assumes that only historical data about the rate of inflation are relevant in the process of building up inflation expectations and that there is no need for additional information regarding elements such as the development of the monetary growth rate. The sluggish and indirect adjustment of the money rate of interest to the changes in the purchasing power of money can be attributed to the phenomenon of money illusion. Fisher writes:

> When prices begin to rise, money interest is scarcely affected. It requires the cumulative effect of a long rise, or a marked rise in prices, to produce a definite advance in the interest rate. If there were no money illusion and if adjustments of interest rates were perfect, unhindered by any failure to foresee future changes in the purchasing power of money or by custom or law or any other impediment, we should have found a very different set of facts (1930, p. 44).

Summarizing it may be stated that Fisher has assumed in his theoretical explanations that the real economic environment is characterized by "imperfect foresight" and moreover that the economic agents are subjected to money illusion. The expected rate of inflation, built up on the basis of historical data, is passed on in the nominal rate of interest gradually and rather sluggishly. This adjustment process goes on through the following two channels. On the one side there exists an adaptive expectations procedure, a learning process, by which, according to the forecast error, the expected rate of inflation and so the money rate of interest are adjusted gradually (price-expectations effect). On the other side there is an indirect adjustment process through the influence of the rate of inflation on the real rate of interest and economic activity and the concomitant induced demand for credit (credit-market effect). The practical meaning of the difference between the nominal and the real rate of interest arises from the sluggish adjustment process, by which a higher rate of inflation can influence the real variables in the economy temporarily.

In his well-known book *Value and capital* Hicks (1939) also devoted much attention to the influence of changes in price expectations on the course of the economic process. This theory is dynamic to the extent that the temporary equilibrium is governed by expectations. Hicks especially analyses the effect of actual prices on price expectations and distinguishes between the influence of present prices and the influence of past observed prices. In this context he states that if the influence of the given past prices dominates, the price expectations can be treated as given data. Hicks introduces the notion of "the elasticity of expectations" and makes a distinction between the rigidly inelastic expectations (price expectations are given from the past) on the one hand and a unit elasticity of expectations (expected prices change in the same direction and in the same proportion as current prices) on the other hand. With regard to the extreme case of an elasticity of expectations greater than one Hicks remarks "The elasticity of expectations will be greater than unity, if a change in current prices makes people feel that they can recognize a trend, so that they try to extrapolate . . ." (1939, pp. 204–205). In this way expectations can be moulded, according to various possible rules, by actual experience in combinations of periods in the past.

Hahn also analyses the influence of expectations in the context of the equilibrium theory and of the dynamic stability conditions. He examines the types of expectations which must be postulated in order for dynamic equilibrium to be possible. In Hahn's opinion the existence of equilibrium through time presupposes the existence of an expectation function of constant form. This function relates expected events to past events. He speaks about "plastic" expectations when he criticizes models assuming that any price that is established will be regarded as permanent. Hahn states, however, "This assumption seems to me entirely unwarranted, and incidentally precludes the action of what economists have for long regarded as one of the main stabilizing forces in the system – namely 'normal expectations'" (1952, pp. 816–817). In our opinion Hahn can be considered as a predecessor of the semi-rational expectations analysis (see Section 6.4) when he postulates: "As long as the variations in demand are systematic and not random it is possible *to learn by experience* and thus to involve a 'rule of thumb' or a mode of routine behaviour which will ensure that the output forthcoming at the planned price is exactly sold" (1952, p. 804).

After the Second World War attempts were regularly made to cope with the psychologically determined expectations with regard to economic variables in macroeconomic models in a more appropriate way. At first it was simply guessing at the way in which individual economic agents build up their expectations in practice. In this process attempts were always made to trace a quantitative representation of this economic behaviour. However in this context it rapidly appeared that the individuals in shaping their inflation expectations made use of the actual rates of inflation in the past, as Fisher and Hicks pointed out in their publications in the thirties. It is Cagan, one of the modern authors in this field, who has elaborated Fisher's expectations procedure further in a theoretical way through the introduction of an "adaptive expectations function". In his theoretical explanations he assumes that the demand for money (in a situation of hyperinflation) is negatively related to the expected rate of inflation, which is brought out by a distributed-lag (adaptive-behaviour) function (Cagan 1956).[2]

In this more or less mechanical expectations theory it is supposed that inflationary expectations are formed by an extrapolation of the rates of inflation from the past. The expected rate of inflation is a weighted average of the actual rate of inflation and the observed inflation rates from the past, whereby the weights are declining as they concern inflation rates further in the past. According to the present forecast error the economic agents will continually revise and adjust the expected rate of inflation for the future period. In this expectations procedure it is mostly assumed that the public is not knowledgeable regarding the economic forces which dominate the variable to be predicted. In these circumstances the inflationary expectations, based on irrational behaviour, will systematically diverge from the rate of inflation which is generated by the theoretical model. This adaptive expectations hypothesis, which has recently come to the fore in theoretical and empirical studies, will be considered in detail in Section 4.3 in relation to the shifting Phillips-curve analysis.

---

2. The theory of adaptive expectations is also applied in many empirical studies, e.g. Gibson (1970), Siebke and Willms (1972), Yohe and Karnosky (1969), and Lahiri (1976).

4. From a non-monetary to a monetary Phillips curve

4.1. The orthodox unemployment-inflation trade-off

The theoretical relation between inflation and unemployment, which was given a central position in macroeconomic theory just after the Second World War upon the introduction of the Phillips curve, essentially finds its origin in the publications of Hume (1741). This author has pointed out that a change in the money supply will initially give rise to a change in the level of production and employment and will subsequently result in a change in wages and prices (money stimulates trade doctrine). Fisher (1926) was also involved in the study of this empirical phenomenon which was given a detailed analysis by Phillips 32 years later (Phillips 1958). Fisher remarks in his empirical study that an inflationary situation in the economy has an attendant low level of unemployment and high level of economic activity while a slumping business cycle and a concomitant high level of unemployment are rather associated with a deflationary environment. Essentially he describes a dynamic process, initiated by unexpected changes in nominal expenditures, whereby he makes a distinction between high and low prices on the one hand and an increase and a decrease of the price level on the other hand. This distinction links up closely with the central ultimate goal of monetary policy at the time, namely the stabilization of the purchasing power of money. Fisher uses the rate of change of the price level as the independent variable which sets the dynamic process going, whereby the level of employment appears as the dependent variable. In this context he notices:

> When the dollar is losing value, or in other words when the price level is rising, a business man finds his receipts rising as fast, on the average, as this general rise of prices, but not his expenses; because his expenses consist, to a large extent, of things which are contractually fixed.... Employment is then stimulated – for a time at least (Fisher 1926, p. 787).

From the publication of Fisher it appears (A) that he clearly distinguishes the trade-off between inflation and unemployment in the short run; and (B) that he already speaks implicitly about the significance of the distinction between expected and unexpected changes in the price level for the course of the economic process. The theoretical view which is the basis of (A) was elaborated in more detail by Phillips in the fifties, while Friedman's critical remarks on Phillips curve analysis in the sixties were based on the distinction mentioned in (B). Since Phillips's publication (1958), the traditional trade-off between inflation and unemployment has had a substantial influence in economics in a theoretical as well as in a practical way. The Phillips curve has been considered in the literature many times to be Keynesian macroeconomic theory's "missing equation", which would determine the division of a change in nominal income into price and quantity components and would also link up the real and the monetary sectors of the economy.

Summarizing we may conclude that the view which was the basis of the original Phillips curve involves, as it were, an amalgamation of elements of the Keynesian demand-pull inflation theory on the one hand and of the income or cost-push inflation theory on the other hand. The original shape of the empirically determined Phillips curve points out the direct negative relation between the rate of increase of nominal wages and the rate of unemployment (or changes in it), whereby the latter rate can be considered as the expression of the disequilibrium situation in the labour market. In the conceptions of the demand-pull and cost-push inflation theories the two variables, employment and the development of nominal wages, are considered to be quite independent of each other. However consideration of the Phillips curve serves to emphasize that in reality there exists a sound interrelation between the employment situation and the development of nominal wages and prices.[1] Next the original Phillips curve was converted into the negative relation between the rate of inflation and the rate of unemployment, through a correction of the rate of increase of nominal wages by the average rate of growth of labour productivity. This conversion is very useful for policy makers because it is possible for them to determine the costs in terms of unemployment when they have a special target with regard to the purchasing power of money (and conversely).

Algebraically the orthodox trade-off can be rendered as $\pi = \gamma X$, where X represents the aggregate excess demands on the goods market and on the labour market and π is the actual rate of inflation. The coefficient γ represents the numerical value of the trade-off between the rate of inflation and the disequilibrium situation on the goods and labour markets. This equation is popularly used among policy makers as a stable social choice, in which there exist known and alternative combinations of inflation and unemployment which may be chosen.

The above mentioned view, involving a trade-off between inflation and unemployment in the short run, was generally the framework within which the macroeconomic-policy decision-making process took place in the different countries until the mid-sixties. Policy makers always assumed in their stabilization policy that there would exist a consistent and stable trade-off between money erosion and the employment level. However the publications of Friedman (1969b) and Phelps (1972a) gradually changed the minds of policy makers, who recognized the

1. This view is based on Okun's Law, according to which there exists an empirical relation between the excess demand on the goods market (the rate of capacity utilization) and the excess demand on the labour market, in the sense that the rate of unemployment decreases when the rate of capacity utilization increases, and conversely (Okun 1962). From Okun's empirical studies it has appeared that the employment elasticity of production for the United States economy is equal to a third. This means that an annual rate of growth of production of three per cent above the trend value, arising from a change in expenditures, would result in a decrease of one per cent in the rate of unemployment and vice versa.

limitations of monetary and fiscal policy in solving this policy dilemma. Since that time policy makers have been more and more in doubt about the validity of Phillips curve analysis. This sceptical attitude in the last decade was brought about by the following considerations. Statistical studies have shown that some economic variables, such as the development of business profits, the power of trade unions, the dispersion of the balance between unemployment and unfilled vacancies on different markets, and so on, also influence the shape and stability of the curve. This means that in the course of time a great number of different curves can be distinguished according as more variables which may influence the relation between inflation and unemployment are taken into consideration. Consequently the short-run curve will gradually shift when these variables are changing. In the recent past in this context inflation expectations and the concomitant "inflation psychology" played a crucial role in the ultimate course of the economic process. Especially in the seventies it could be observed in practice that the acceleration of inflation increased together with an unchanged and sometimes even a rising rate of unemployment (stagflation phenomenon).

Friedman's alternative theoretical viewpoint, mentioned above, presented in his famous address to the American Economic Association, has drawn much attention in the economic literature. This theory is identified in recent monetary theoretical publications as the "natural unemployment rate hypothesis", the "expectations-augmented Phillips curve" or the "accelerationist hypothesis". In these more or less coherent conceptions the neoclassical thesis emerges that in the long run there is no relation between changes in the general price level and the real economic variables in the economy, so that there exists a neutrality of money. In other words in the long run the purported trade-off between inflation and unemployment will disappear, although in the short run, in the transition period, a higher rate of inflation will generate positive effects in the real sector of the economy. The long run points to a situation characterized by a macroeconomic equilibrium whereby a possible difference between the actual and the expected rate of inflation is completely eliminated. Friedman finds empirical support for his theoretical view in the Brazilian inflation in the early sixties. Friedman remarks in his address

> Suppose . . . everyone anticipates that prices rise at the rate of more than 75 per cent a year – as, for example, Brazilians did a few years ago. Then wages must rise at that rate simply to keep real wages unchanged. . . . When Brazil embarked on a policy to bring down the rate of price rise, and succeeded in bringing the price rise down to about 45 per cent a year, there was a sharp initial rise in unemployment because, under the influence of earlier anticipations wages kept rising, at a pace that was higher than the new rate of price rise, though lower than earlier (1969b, p. 102).

In this quotation it is clearly shown that in a strong inflationary environment economic agents are progressively less liable to the money-illusion phenomenon and take their economic decisions on the basis of the actual and expected inflationary process. Friedman and Phelps, in their critical remarks on the orthodox Phillips curve, clearly pointed out that the demand and supply relations in the different markets are dependent on the (expected) relative prices rather than on the nominal or general money prices.

In the next section an analysis will be given of the impact of these inflation expectations on the traditional trade-off problem. At the same time an explanation will be put forward of how the theoretical views of Friedman and Phelps gave the incentive to a more dynamic analysis of the trade-off phenomenon.

4.2. The expectations-augmented Phillips curve

Although it was in the sixties that the significance of inflation expectations with regard to the trade-off problem was strongly emphasized in economic literature, attention had already paid to this question earlier. Lerner writes: "What is harmful about inflation is not the rise in prices but the failure to anticipate and offset them. . . . the essential element . . . is the disappointment of expectations" (1949, p. 194; see also Von Mises 1924). In the last decade many industrialized countries have been confronted in the long run with a more or less unchanged employment situation and a concomitant different rate of inflation, which is opposed to the traditional view as was presented in the preceding section. Friedman and Phelps have always pointed out in their publications that differences between nominal or money prices on the one hand and real or relative prices on the other play a critical role in the decision-making process of the economic subjects. When assuming a monetary-oriented Phillips curve it is necessary to take account of the importance of inflation expectations explicitly. The authors mentioned above have set forth their theoretical views about Phillips curve analysis with an explicit introduction of inflation expectations. Their theoretical model focuses on three issues, namely the natural unemployment rate hypothesis, the accelerated rate of inflation and the adaptive expectations hypothesis (Friedman 1969b; Phelps 1967).[2]

The expectations-augmented Phillips curve can be rendered algebraically as follows:

$$\pi = \gamma X + \alpha\pi^*, \quad \gamma > 0, \quad 0 < \alpha \leqslant 1 \tag{1}$$

where π = the actual rate of inflation;
π^* = the expected rate of inflation;
X = the reformulated excess-demand variable, which is the difference between the natural and the actual rate of unemployment ($U_N - U_F$) and measures the disequilibrium situation on the goods market and on the labour market – as far as the natural rate of unemployment dominates the actual rate of unemployment ($U_N > U_F$ and $X > 0$) the inflation rate increases, and conversely;
α = the price expectations coefficient.

The factor γ is essentially a compound parameter, which on the one hand expresses how a change in expenditures is rendered

2. For theoretical reflections about the Phillips curve and the significance of inflation expectations we refer to publications of Laidler (1976) and Trevithick (1976) respectively. See also in this context the detailed review article of Santomoro and Seater (1978).

into a change in the rate of unemployment (Okun's Law) and which on the other hand points out the sensitivity of nominal wages to changes in the unemployment rate. Both effects together will influence the actual rate of inflation and so far the factor γ determines the slope of the curve.

The natural rate of unemployment, determined by structural institutional factors, Friedman defines as follows:

> The "natural rate of unemployment", in other words, is the level that would be ground out by the Walrasian system of general equilibrium equations, provided there is imbedded in them the actual structural characteristics of the labor and commodity markets, including market imperfections, stochastic variability in demands and supplies, the costs of gathering information about job vacancies and labor availabilities, the costs of mobility, and so on (1969b, p. 102).

The natural rate of unemployment, which may sharply differ from one country to another, is mainly determined by factors like the degree of organization of the trade unions, labour mobility, the degree of coordination between demand and supply of labour in a qualitative sense, unemployment benefits, and so on. This natural rate or equilibrium rate of unemployment represents a situation which is consistent with an equilibrium on the goods and labour markets, whereby the excess demand on these markets equals zero. In these circumstances wages are stable, but in a growing economy real wages will rise according to the rate of increase in the average labour productivity. The unemployment rate is "natural" in the sense that it results from unavoidable economic frictions and therefore cannot be considered as an art-product of some traditional monetary policy measure. It is a variable economic factor which can be influenced by government interventions with regard to the structure and working of the labour markets – education programmes, labour-market information, and so on (see Friedman 1975b; Prescott 1975; and Frisch 1977). The concept of the natural unemployment rate is aimed at dividing the monetary and non-monetary aspects of the employment situation, as Wicksell did with regard to the rate of interest.

The equation mentioned above points out that the actual rate of inflation will be higher the higher the expected rate of inflation of economic agents and the lower the actual rate of unemployment (a higher excess demand on the goods market and on the labour market). If the price expectations coefficient is assumed to be equal to zero, or indeed if $0 < \alpha < 1$, the original Phillips curve results, whereby economic agents are subject to a complete or a partial money illusion.[3] As far as $\alpha = 1$ and with fully anticipated inflation ($\pi = \pi^*$), the actual rate of unemployment (U_F) is in accordance with the natural rate of unemployment (U_N) and the conventional trade-off between inflation and unemployment will disappear. In this long-run equilibrium situation, when there is no money illusion with regard to the demand and supply equations and only expected relative prices and the expected real income are important, the following relation holds:

$$\gamma X = 0 \quad \text{and} \quad U_N = U_F \tag{2}$$

In these circumstances the current natural rate of unemployment is consistent with any rate of inflation as far as this rate is fully anticipated by the economic agents.[4]

Equation (1) can also be rendered in a more general form as follows:

$$\pi = F(X, \pi^*) \tag{3}$$

This equation means that the actual rate of inflation is dependent on the actual employment situation as well as on the expected rate of inflation built up by the economic subjects. The mutual macroeconomic relations are represented graphically in Figure 1, assuming a linear shape of the Phillips curve.

---

3. Neo-Keynesian authors rather consider the factor α as an expression of the power of trade-unions in using a change of the expected rate of inflation to influence changes in the nominal wage rate (see Tobin 1972).

4. Assuming that the actual rate of inflation equals the expected rate of inflation ($\pi = \pi^*$), it results from equation (1) that $\pi(1-\alpha) = \gamma X$, so that a long-run trade-off only exists as far as $\alpha < 1$. Empirical studies have shown that before 1971 the price expectations coefficient in a great number of countries in the Western industrialized world had a value less than one, while after 1971 this value is equal to one (see Gordon 1972; Laidler and Parkin 1975; and Sargent 1971).

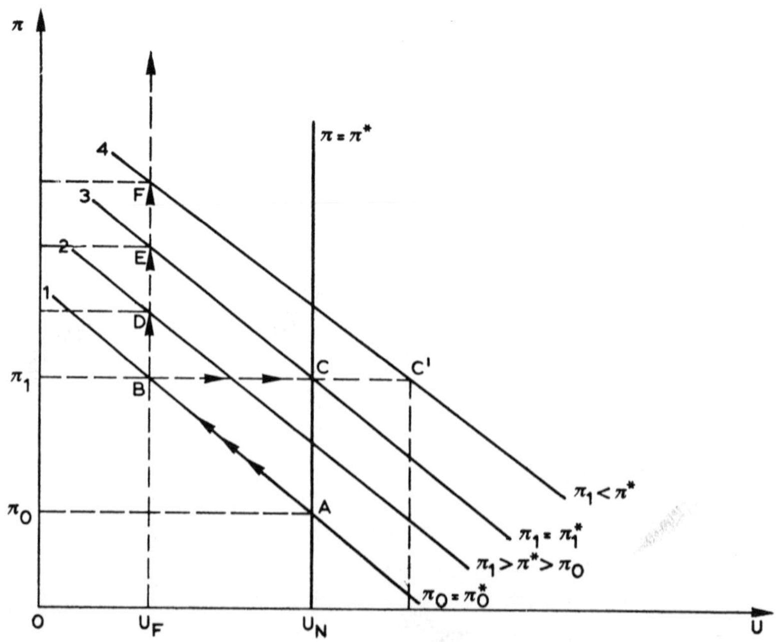

Figure 1.

The short-run Phillips curves in the figure refer to given inflation expectations, whereby, in more technical terms, a given curve is located further from the origin as it involves a higher expected rate of inflation. According to equation (2) the long-run curve is a vertical line at the natural rate of unemployment (U_N). In these circumstances the expected rate of inflation has become equal to the actual rate of inflation and economic agents have no incentive to change their economic decisions. This vertical Phillips curve renders all the combinations of the actual rate of inflation (π) and the natural unemployment rate (U_N) which are consistent with a fully anticipated inflation by the economic subjects ($\pi = \pi^*$ and $\alpha = 1$). In this situation Phelps talks about a macroeconomic equilibrium and declares:

> Then households will not exhibit any systematic tendency to regret their job acceptance/rejection decisions, or wish that they had found different product suppliers on whom to bestow their patronage. Likewise, firms on

the whole will not feel any systematic regret or surprise at the results of their price and wage setting for the attraction of new customers and employers (1972a, p. 38).

From the preceding explanations it has appeared that there exists a relation between the disequilibrium situation on the goods market and the disequilibrium situation on the labour market through Okun's Law. Both are determining the development of the actual rate of inflation. It is interesting with the help of the figure to analyse the process through which an expansive monetary impulse influences the economic activity. Starting from a macroeconomic equilibrium in point A (U_N, π_0), where the actual rate of inflation equals the expected rate of inflation ($\pi_0 = \pi_0^*$), an expansive monetary impulse or nominal demand pull will generate the following price and quantity adjustment process. At first, consequent on an increase in the utilization rate, the rate of unemployment will fall (U_F) and the actual rate of inflation will rise according to the induced excess demands on the goods market and on the labour market (π_1). As the expected rate of inflation is initially unchanged (π_0^*) so the short-run Phillips curve (1) is of immediate interest, and a movement along the curve (to point B) is brought about. However in the long run the positive difference between the actual and the expected rate of inflation cannot be maintained continuously, so that ultimately the impact on the real sector of the economy is removed. For in course of time the economic agents will adjust their price expectations upwards quite quickly and will incorporate these changed inflation expectations in their economic dispositions (wage negotiations). In this context Friedman points out: "Comparisons among countries . . . as well as other tests, seem so far entirely consistent with what any reasonable man must surely expect: which is that, since you can't fool all the people all the time, the true long-run Phillips curve is vertical" (1975a, p. 28).[5]

The adjustment process mentioned above, through which the curve ultimately shifts to the right (from B to C), resulting from the gradual adjustment of inflation expectations and the in-

5. See also Laidler (1978), and Friedman (1976, ch. 12).

duced changes in the decisions of the economic agents, can be rendered as follows. The individual entrepreneur, confronted with a rise in total monetary demand, will interpret the changed market situation as a fortuitous increase in the demand for his own product at current prices. This unexpected increase in demand will be considered as a relative, that is, a specific change in demand. If the change in demand was accordingly related to the supplier's specific market situation in the past, the current increase will be more strongly interpreted by the supplier in his own favour, and thus will only be considered as a general increase in demand to a slight measure. The uncertainty with regard to the changed market situation means that the entrepreneur-supplier does not adjust his price initially because of the costs involved (costs of information, catalogues, costs of advertising, and so on), but first of all will bring about a quantity adjustment. This means that because of imperfect market information the expansive monetary impulse will at first result in an adjustment of production and only in a later stage, when it appears that the change in demand had a more general character, in a price adjustment. In this context Lucas remarks: "All formulations of the natural rate theory postulate rational agents, whose decisions depend on relative prices only, placed in an economic setting in which they cannot distinguish relative from general price movements" (Lucas 1973, p. 327; see also Arak 1977b).

In his theoretical explanations about the business cycle Lucas assumes that economic agents are rational and act in conformity with the market situation. This means that they are guided in their economic decision making by relative price movements and that they build up their inflation expectations in an efficient and rational way. However the difficulty is that the market participants cannot distinguish between relative price movements on the one hand and movements of the general price level on the other hand. In these circumstances a rise of a single price or wage rate will be interpreted partially as a relative price rise of a product or of a factor of production on a special market (a change in the relative price and wage structure). From this point of view the Phillips curve has to be interpreted in a way other than traditionally was the case. This means that this curve points out what amount of employment is generated by a given difference between the actual and the expected price level. The causality which underlies Lucas's view and which is opposed to the orthodox Phillips curve analysis is closely linked up with the views already pointed out by Fisher's publication in 1926. Thus in Lucas's model unexpected increases in the price level boost aggregate supply, the reason being that suppliers of labour and goods mistakenly interpret surprise increases in the aggregate price level as increases in the relative prices of the labour and goods they are supplying. To what extent the supply of goods and employment will react as a result of the difference between the actual and the expected rate of inflation is dependent on the change in the general price level in relation to the relative price movement. When relative price movement is slight, a change in a particular price will be considered by the market participants as an indication of a general price movement. Consequently a slight quantity adjustment will take place. Conversely when the relative price movement is substantial, such a movement will give little information about the development of the general price level, and so substantial quantity adjustments with regard to the real variables will arise (Parkin 1978a).

Consequent on the behaviour of the entrepreneur-supplier, as described above, an initial improvement of the rate of utilization will increase the demand for labour. Because of the imperfect information on the labour market the individual employee makes the same error of interpretation and interprets the initial nominal wage increase as a relative real-wage improvement. He assumes that prices and other wages have not increased in the same measure and therefore that his relative real income position has improved.

This interesting windfall will induce employees, who, with a certain acceptable wage rate in mind, try to find a better job on the labour market by job-searching activities, to stop this search process prematurely (the marginal costs of information and search having increased). And indeed the upswing in economic activity increases the chance that an unemployed searcher will find a job with a wage rate higher than or equal to his reservation wage rate. This behaviour of employees therefore means a reduction of the unemployment rate, since the voluntary or search unemployment decreases (Mortensen 1970; Hall 1979).[6] Moreover the recruitment process of labour is fostered, because the entrepreneurs, consequent on the increased economic activity, will be very busy on the labour market in recruiting activities. Besides employment will also increase because in the upswing of the business cycle prices of goods rise faster than nominal wage rates, through which a relative fall in real wages arises. Friedman expresses this in the following way:

> Because selling prices of products typically respond to an unanticipated rise in nominal demand faster than prices of factors of production, real wages received have gone down – though real wages anticipated by employees went up since employees implicitly evaluated the wages offered at the earlier price level. Indeed, the simultaneous fall *ex post* in real wages to employers and rise *ex ante* in real wages to employees is what enabled employment to increase (1969b, p. 104; see also Kareken 1978 and Friedman 1977).

From this quotation and the reactions of employers and employees on the initial expansive monetary impulse, it appears that there exists a movement along the short-run Phillips curve (see Figure 1, curve 1). This behaviour is essentially based on a certain asymmetry with regard to the sources of price information and on a misinterpretation of the current economic situation. The employee knows the nominal wage rate offered to him before he knows the price level and therefore he anticipates an improvement of real wages. The employer in his turn knows the price of his product before he knows the wage rate he has to pay, so he anticipates a fall in real wages (Hall 1975). In a world of uncertainty market participants are deceived through a "surprise inflation" and take wrong and often disadvantageous economic decisions on the basis of misinterpretations with regard to the market situation. Hall puts it pithily as follows:

---

6. Hall concludes that "under plausible assumptions the natural rate is independent of the supply or demand for labor. Only the costs of recruiting, the costs of turnover to employees, the efficiency of matching jobs and workers and the costs of unemployment to workers are likely to influence the natural rate of unemployment strongly". (Hall 1979, p. 153).

> the benefits of inflation derive from the use of expansionary policy to *trick* economic agents into behaving in socially preferable ways even though their behavior is not in their own interest. . . . The gap between actual and expected inflation measures the extent of the trickery. The optimal policy is not nearly as expansionary when expectations adjust rapidly, and most of the effect of an inflationary policy is dissipated in costly anticipated inflation (1976, p. 141).

However the discrepancy between the actual and the expected rate of inflation ($\pi_1 - \pi_0^*$) will give rise to a revision and an adaptation of the incorrect price and wage expectations when in course of time more information becomes available. When the entrepreneur-supplier perceives that the general price level has risen and that the increase in demand has a more general character, he will adapt his inflation expectations and increase the price of the product. In the same way it holds that when employees realize that the increase in demand is more general, they will extend their searching activities on the labour market and try to adapt their wages to the higher actual rate of inflation to secure ultimately their real income position. The employees attempt to protect themselves against the erosion of the purchasing power of the nominal wages by claiming higher money wages (the reservation wage-rate will be adapted).

Because institutionally wages are determined periodically by contract the expected rate of inflation is extremely important in the wage negotiations process, for to make decisions about the increase in nominal wage rates it is important to know what will be the rate of inflation, aiming at a target with regard to the real wage rate. Extending and lengthening the duration of the search processes on the labour market and the adaptation of inflation expectations will give rise to a gradual elimination of the original improvement in employment. Supposing a lag in the nominal wage adjustment Friedman states "the decline *ex post* in real wages will soon come to affect anticipations. Employees start to reckon on rising prices of the things they buy and to demand higher nominal wages for the future" (1969b, p. 104).

As far as the expected rate of inflation exceeds the actual rate of inflation ($\pi^* > \pi_1$) during the adjustment process, a rate of unemployment surpassing the "natural" rate will emerge temporarily (point C′). The resulting deflationary tendencies will cause a revision of inflationary expectations downwards.

As more information about the actual market situation becomes available and more experience about inflation has been gained an increasing revision and adaptation of the expected rate of inflation will gradually arise. The rate of unemployment will rise and ultimately will stabilize at the institutionally-determined "natural" rate from which the process started. The process of adjustment to the new equilibrium situation (point C in Figure 1) may have a more direct or oscillating character, which is crucially dependent on the specific adjustment mechanism of inflation expectations.[7] The interaction between inflation and unemployment is clearly reduced to a transition phenomenon, whereby in the long run, when expectations and realizations are equal, the initial positive effects with regard to the real economic variables disappear.

In the course of time the economy will gradually adjust to the higher rate of monetary growth, so that ultimately only the actual and the expected rate of inflation have risen (point C in the figure, where $\pi_1 = \pi^*$). The rate of inflation will be stable, neither accelerating nor decelerating, and the "surprise inflation", the difference between the actual and the expected rate of inflation, will be eliminated. In that situation however policy makers may decide again to organize a positive effect on production and employment by further increasing the rate of monetary growth. Then a subsequent adjustment process will be started through which a higher rate of inflation emerges in the new equilibrium situation and so the rate of inflation will accelerate. As far as policy makers try to maintain continuously the actual rate of unemployment below the "natural" rate, aiming at a certain target with regard to employment ($U_F < U_N$), this can only be realized through an acceleration of the rate of monetary growth (the path BDEF in the graph) and a concomitant acceleration of the rate of inflation. This means

7. For a clear theoretical explanation of the dynamic adjustment process, we may refer to Frenkel and Rodriguez (1977). See also Scarth (1977) and Friedman (1978).

that the actual rate of inflation has to anticipate the expected rate of inflation which the employees incorporate in their wage demands continuously, thus the economic agents are permanently deceived. In these circumstances there always exists a "surprise inflation" ($\pi > \pi^*$), generating positive effects with regard to the real variables (the accelerationist hypothesis).

This view of the accelerationists, which essentially involves a combination of the natural rate hypothesis and the adaptive expectations mechanism, can be rendered as follows. Starting from equation (1) and a price expectations coefficient $\alpha = 1$, the relation between the acceleration of the rate of inflation ($\dot{\pi}$) and the rate of growth of the other variables ($\dot{X}$ and $\dot{\pi}^*$) can be represented as follows:

$$\dot{\pi} = \gamma\dot{X} + \dot{\pi}^*. \tag{1'}$$

After substitution of the undermentioned equation which describes the adaptive expectations hypothesis (see Section 4.3), whereby the forecasting error (surprise inflation) is eliminated through a change in the expected rate of inflation: $\dot{\pi}^* = \lambda(\pi - \pi^*)$, from equations (1) and (1′) the following expression results (Humphrey 1978, note, p. 17):

$$\dot{\pi} = \lambda\dot{X} + \gamma\lambda X. \tag{1''}$$

Since in this case the excess demand on the goods market is unchanged ($\dot{X} = 0$) because the authorities aim at a certain amount of employment ($U_F < U_N$), relation (1″) becomes:

$$\dot{\pi} = \gamma\lambda X. \tag{1'''}$$

This means that the conventional trade-off is reduced to a trade-off between the acceleration of the rate of inflation ($\dot{\pi}$) and the excess demand on the goods market and on the labour market (X), for the impact of changes in the rate of monetary growth on the real economic variables is only temporary and the cost of this short-run effect is an acceleration of the process of money erosion.

Summarizing it can be said that implementing and maintaining an inflationary monetary policy will unavoidably give rise to inflationary expectations in the course of time, shifting the short-run Phillips curve to the right. Therefore there will be no long-run exploitable trade-off between inflation and unemployment, but at most a trade-off exists between an accelerating rate of inflation and the rate of unemployment. Within the macroeconomic stabilization policy framework there is rather talk of an intertemporal trade-off problem: either there is less unemployment today, but a higher rate of inflation with the same or a higher rate of unemployment in the future or one must accept more unemployment today to parry the money erosion of tomorrow. A stabilization policy based on the original view of a stable trade-off between inflation and unemployment will fail in the long run and will only result in an institutionalization of the inflation phenomenon without accomplishing a lasting improvement of the employment situation. The economic agents pass through a learning process and will not continue to make forecasting errors. In the course of time they make their decisions rationally and the forecasting errors with regard to the expected rate of inflation will disappear (see Chapter 5). Gradually a greater dispersion of economic information will arise and economic agents become more expert in economics, which promotes the accuracy of inflation expectations. Empirical studies have shown that the adjustment coefficient, measuring the reaction of the public on the current expectational error, varies with the numerical value and the change in the actual rate of inflation (Khan 1977; see also Grosseschmidt 1976; and Faulwasser 1979). This means that the adjustment of the expected rate of inflation will come about ever faster, so that the long run becomes ever shorter and will ultimately lie within the horizon relevant for economic policy. In these circumstances Keynes's celebrated pronouncement has to be modified as follows: "In the long run we are not all dead".

The natural rate hypothesis and the accelerationists' view have two implications for macroeconomic stabilization policy, in this case for monetary policy. Insofar as monetary authorities aim at a certain target of employment (U_F), they will ultimately lose their grip on monetary stability because the rate of inflation will eventually accelerate when the actual rate of unemployment is being maintained below the natural rate. However when a stabilization of the rate of inflation is preferred (π_0 or π_1), the rate of unemployment will rise in the course of time to the natural rate at any equilibrium value of the rate of inflation ($\pi = \pi^*$). Therefore monetary-policy activism can achieve temporarily a short-run benefit in terms of a rise in employment and production but at the cost of more inflation in the long run. When the rate of time preference of economic subjects is high, the preference for such policy activism and the concomitant short-run benefits will be strong. As has already been said many times this policy is only effective insofar as the individual economic agents can be deceived to make suboptimal decisions as a consequence of imperfect information about monetary policy rules.

4.3. The adaptive expectations analysis ("error-learning-hypothesis")

From the explanations in the preceding section it appears that an introduction of inflationary expectations into the Phillips curve model is very important for the ultimate course of the economic process and also clears the way for a dynamic approach of the trade-off problem. However the question still remains to be answered through which procedure economic agents build up their expectations with respect to the rate of inflation.

Naturally it is possible to form a notion of these expectations in a more direct way by setting up an inquiry with important market participants. Since 1947 Livingston has made a twice-yearly inquiry in the United States with a relatively small group of economists in business and in the academic world into their expectations with regard to the development (the coming 6-to-12 months) of some strategic macroeconomic variables, included the rate of inflation. Based on this information it might be possible to make a reasonable forecast of the expected rate of inflation. Afterwards some economists made use of Livingston's published results in their empirical studies about the expected rate of inflation and the development of the nominal interest rate and the nominal wage rate (Gibson 1972; Turnovsky and

Wachter 1972). More recently Carlson (1977) has traced how unbiased the forecasts of Livingston with regard to price expectations have been. He comes to the conclusion that in a period of 29 years (58 surveys) there was a "surprise inflation" in 45 cases (the actual rate of inflation exceeding the expected rate of inflation) and only in 13 cases the expected rate of inflation was overestimated (see also Mullineaux 1977a,1977b). Next to this direct expectations procedure based on gathering information from the economic agents, until recently the procedure mostly used started from the hypothesis that the public will build up its inflation expectations on the basis of past experiences. As was pointed out in Chapter 3, Cagan, in analysing the demand for money in periods of hyperinflation "constructed", for want of something better, an expected rate of inflation. He made use then of a specific and a rather arbitrary transformation of actual rates of inflation from the past according to the theory of adaptive expectations. Corresponding to this expectations hypothesis economic agents, confronted with a lack of information in an uncertain economic world, base their inflationary expectations on a weighted sum of the actual rates of inflation from the past. If the actual rate of inflation diverges from the expected value a fraction of the forecasting error ("surprise inflation") will find expression in a revision and adaptation of the expected rate of inflation with respect to the next period. This adjustment process, whereby the inflation from the past is extrapolated, has a rather mechanical characteristic and can be rendered discretely as follows:

$$\pi_t^* - \pi_{t-1}^* = \lambda(\pi_{t-1} - \pi_{t-1}^*), \quad 0 < \lambda < 1. \tag{1}$$

in which λ is an adjustment coefficient and π_{t-1} and π_{t-1}^* represent the actual and the expected rates of inflation in the previous period. This equation means that the expected rate of inflation will be adjusted proportionally, according to the prediction error in the last period. When the actual rate of inflation is underestimated or overestimated, then the expected rate of inflation will be revised and adapted upwards or downwards respectively. For the sake of simplicity in the following explanations a linear adjustment process will be postulated. This adaptive expectations hypothesis may involve an irrational forecasting behaviour, and in certain circumstances this mechanism can generate predictions which are systematically inaccurate. When monetary authorities pursue monetary policy behaviour in such a way that the rate of inflation accelerates continuously, an expectations model based only on observed inflation rates from the past will forecast an expected rate of inflation which is underestimated consistently (see Section 4.2). This means a systematic underestimation of the rate of inflation so that the maintenance of this hypothesis, notwithstanding the continuous mistakes, reflects irrational behaviour on the part of the economic agents (see Chapter 5).

The supposition of systematic forecasting errors is justified when there exists an unexpected rate of inflation continuously, fluctuating in an erratic way, so that no long-term development of the variable concerned can be observed. In these circumstances monetary authorities must be very ingenious to organize such a monetary policy that a certain "surprise inflation", an expectational error, arises. In this situation, of imperfect information with respect to monetary policy behaviour, there is no basis for building up inflationary expectations rationally. Therefore from sheer necessity expectations must be built up in an irrational way. In this context Phelps points out:

> Hence if new men take over the conduct of the nation's monetary policy who have unheard-of objectives for the path of the inflation rate, one cannot plausibly assume that their moves will be correctly anticipated on the average by the population at large. In this sort of situation, where a new policy is introduced, the notion of adaptive expectations seems to be the order of the day almost by default (1972a, p. 48).

According to the equation of the learning-process approach (1), the expected rate of inflation is an exponentially weighted average of the past observed rates of inflation, with decreasing weights according to the more distant past. With the aid of equation (1) the expected rate of inflation in this period can be described as a linear combination of the actual and the expected rate of inflation in the previous period.

$$\pi_t^* = \lambda\pi_{t-1} + (1-\lambda)\pi_{t-1}^* \qquad (2)$$

When the second term in this equation is substituted continuously a geometric progression results, in which the expected rate of inflation can be rendered as a weighted sum of all inflation rates in the past and the sum of the weights is equal to one. Solving equation (2) gives the following result:

$$\pi_t^* = \lambda \sum_{i=1}^{\infty} (1-\lambda)^{i-1} \pi_{t-i}, \quad 0 < \lambda < 1. \tag{3}$$

The weights λ, $\lambda(1-\lambda)$, $\lambda(1-\lambda)^2$, and so on, give expression of the extent to which the past observed rates of inflation determine the current expected rate of inflation. The speed at which the weights decrease is, as it were, dependent on the "length of the memory" of economic agents with respect to the inflation in the past. When the weights are decreasing very rapidly ($\lambda \to 1$) it essentially means that economic agents have a "short memory", so that recent rates of inflation dominate the adjustment process. However when the weights are decreasing rather slowly ($\lambda \to 0$), economic agents have a "long memory", so that the current expected rate of inflation is influenced substantially through the rates of inflation further in the past.[8]

Critical authors have pointed out that the adaptive expectations hypothesis represents naive and rather mechanical behaviour with respect to the inflationary expectations, because economic agents are assumed only to take into account past observed inflation rates. Moreover it is assumed that the weights are constant and independent of the current economic situation and economic policy pursued (Lucas 1973, pp. 326–331). All this means that economic agents take no account of all the other factors, such as the past rate of monetary growth, the expected rate of monetary growth, and so on, which also determine the development of the rate of inflation and which, if considered, might reduce the forecasting errors. These critical authors suggest that a "learning process" according to which

8. According to this adjustment mechanism the most recent rates of inflation get the highest weight in the process. If $\lambda = 0.50$, then $\sum_{i=1}^{7} (1-\lambda)^{i-1} = 0.99$, which means that in this case for all practical purposes the weighting could be restricted to seven periods (see Humphrey 1978, p. 16).

the adaptive behaviour of the public with respect to inflationary expectations is built on past observed inflation rates is not rational insofar as besides these there is additional information available which could improve price forecasts (Arak 1977a, pp. 1–30; Humphrey 1978 p. 18). Mullineaux's empirical studies with regard to the United States have shown that information about monetary growth rates in the past and about the current expected rate of money growth was an important factor in explaining inflationary expectations in the 1948–1975 period (1977a, p. 15). This study supports Lucas's statement that the structure of the economic model and the parameters concerned are crucially dependent on the economic policy pursued (see Section 6.2). Especially after 1966 the influence of the expected rate of monetary growth on inflationary expectations was strengthened.

In economic literature it has been pointed out many times that it is difficult to justify the theory that economic agents build up their inflationary expectations according to a procedure which is not consistent with the real inflation-generating process. As has previously been noted, the "learning-process" approach involves a systematic overestimation or underestimation of the actual rate of inflation, which means that the rational, calculating, economic agents will abandon this expectations procedure in the course of time. For assuming an accelerated rate of inflation ($U_F < U_N$ and $\pi > \pi^*$), according to the adaptive expectations hypothesis the actual rate of inflation will be underestimated systematically, resulting in a continuous positive "surprise inflation". When the economic agents perceive these forecasting errors all the time, making expectational errors continuously, they will change their behaviour with regard to building up their inflationary expectations as soon as possible. The "learning procedure" will be abandoned, and they will establish an expectations hypothesis which can forecast the expected rate of inflation in a more accurate way. This rational-expectations hypothesis, which is in accordance with the rational behaviour of the economic subjects, basing inflationary expectations on all the factors determining the actual inflationary process, will be presented in the following chapter.

5. The theory of rational expectations ("rational-expectations hypothesis")

5.1. Assumptions

In economic sciences a revolutionary development in the theory of the construction of expectations regarding economic variables arose with the publication of Muth's paper (1961), which develops an expectations theory assuming rational maximization behaviour on the part of economic agents.[1] The example chosen by Muth to illustrate the formation of rational expectations is rather unsuitable, because it concerns a very special case, namely a model with one exogenous variable (a stochastic disturbance term). In these circumstances the rational inflationary expectations appear to be of an essentially adaptive nature. For here the rational expectation of the future price of the good concerned is only dependent on the prices in the past and the information about the market structure is only important in determining the weights which transform the historic prices into the expected price (Rutledge 1974, pp. 12–16;

1. Muth's publication refers to a variant of the well-known cobweb theorem, originally meant to describe the price-fixing behaviour on certain markets in the agriculture sector. Muth starts from the conception of rational expectations, whereby the demand for goods is dependent on the actual price, while the supply is dependent on the expected price and a random term (influence of the weather). Walters (1971) uses the concept of "consistent expectations" in his model and aims at expectations which are consistent with the relevant economic theory. This means that the suppositions on which the expectations procedure is based are the same as those usually assumed in describing the microeconomic behaviour of economic agents. See in this context also Pashigiani (1970).

Pesando 1976). Still Muth's publication has provided a fundamental incentive to abandon the established tradition, whereby expectations are built up by extrapolating the past observed values of the economic variable concerned. This adaptive or auto-regressive expectations procedure could only be considered as "rational" when it might appear that it is merely the past observed inflation rates which determine price-fixing behaviour.

The important contribution of Muth's theoretical expositions, closely connected with Keynes's views in the *Treatise on money* is as follows. Economic agents are stimulated to gather information about the structure and behaviour of the economic factors which generate the value of the variable to be forecast. When for instance the economic situation is such that an increase in the money supply always results, whether with a distributed lag or not, in a change in the price level in the same direction, it will be to the advantage of the public to take into account this information, about the empirical regularity between the money supply and the price level, in building up their inflationary expectations. For economic agents making use of this information will forecast the expected rate of inflation more precisely and therefore make relatively profitable economic decisions, chargeable to those who omit the relevant information concerned in their decision-making process. Walters (1973, pp. 273–274) speaks in this context about "profit-maximizing expectations".

According to Muth (1961, p. 316) there is a formal agreement between the predictions of academic economists and investors and he points out,

> I should like to suggest that expectations, since they are informed predictions of future events, are essentially the same as the predictions of the relevant economic theory. At the risk of confusing this purely descriptive hypothesis with a pronouncement as to what firms ought to do, we call such expectations "rational". . . . The hypothesis can be rephrased a little more precisely as follows: that expectations of firms (or, more generally, the subjective probability distributions of outcomes) tend to be distributed, for the same information set, about the prediction of the theory (or the "objective" probability distributions of outcomes).

In this quotation it is clearly expressed that expectations about the economic variable can be considered as rational when they are an optimal prediction of the variables concerned. Here it is assumed that economic agents make use of all the relevant available information about the factors which, according to the economic theory, determine the actual development of the economic variable to be forecast. Rationalists postulate that there exists an objective probability distribution with regard to the rate of inflation and the other variables of the model and that economic agents behave as if they know this distribution. This essentially means that the public builds up the precise mathematical expected rate of inflation conditional on all information available at the moment when the expectation is formed. Then the expectations completely incorporate all the information implied in the past values of the variable to be predicted. Muth's view implies that economic agents build up their expectations as if they are fully informed of the process which ultimately generates the real outcome of the variable concerned. In these circumstances the expected values can only differ from the corresponding outcomes of the model consequent on forecasting errors which are themselves independent of the variables generating the prediction. This essentially means that unexpected and random shocks, from the real as well as from the monetary sector in the economy, can bring about prediction errors affecting the behaviour of real output. Next it holds that in these circumstances the subjective predictions of the economic variables involved are not consistently worse than the predictions of the model used in the economy, for the same relations between the macroeconomic variables, as rendered by the model, underlie the formation of expectations about the economic variables concerned. In this way expectations are completely endogenous to the model.

A feature of the theory of rational expectations is to the fact that the public sees an advantage to be gained in the efficient gathering of information about the inflation-generating process and about the most important determinants of this inflation process, aiming at a more precise prediction of the expected rate of inflation. Economic agents do not only anticipate the economic development as this is extrapolated from the past, but they also take into account the rules of economic policy of the decision-making authorities, so there exists feedback between the policy targets in the real sector and the concomitant policy reactions. The use of all this knowledge and information, however incomplete it may be, is, following Muth, deemed "rational" by the advocates of this expectations hypothesis.

Next it is postulated that there exists full competition on all markets, which essentially means that market disequilibria are immediately eliminated by the appropriate price and wage adjustments (the Walrasian tâtonnement process). This assumption links up with the view that actual and expected prices will not diverge, which means a direct adjustment of the expected rate of inflation to changes in the actual rate of inflation, resulting in a continuous macroeconomic equilibrium situation, according to Phelps (see Section 4.2).

Within our analysis rational behaviour of economic subjects is further characterized by the following two issues. Firstly it is supposed that the public calculates with relative prices instead of absolute prices. This means that the market participants are not guided in their economic decision-making processes by the nominal but by the real development of the economic variables, that is, they are not susceptible to the common phenomenon of money illusion. Next expectational errors and biased forecasts with respect to future economic developments and their concomitant wrong and unprofitable decisions stimulate the economic agents to base their decisions on all the relevant available information at the decision-making moment. Then the subjective predictions will not systematically diverge from those of the correct theoretical model of the economy. The expectations of the economic subjects "compete", as it were, with the predictions of the relevant economic theory.

In Muth's original publication and in the applications of the rational-expectations hypothesis it is implicitly assumed that gathering and interpreting of information can be achieved immediately and without cost – according to the requirement that all relevant information should be fully incorporated in the rational prediction (Modigliani and Shiller 1973). Sargent makes this supposition more explicit where he points out with regard to the rationality, in the sense used by Muth: "the second hypothesis, namely that readily available information will not be wasted makes sharper tests of the expectations hypothesis possible" (1972, p. 75). Naturally however such a rational behaviour is not costless, which means that gathering additional information by itself involves a choice alternative (see Chapter 6), for the costs connected with the information activities must be weighed against the costs of irrational behaviour, which can be represented by the costs of a less precise prediction of the value of the economic variables concerned and the concomitant wrong decisions.

Summarizing it can be said that the shortcomings of the adaptive expectations hypothesis, finding expression in a consistent underestimation or overestimation of the actual rate of inflation, have given the incentive to the introduction of the rational-expectations hypothesis in Phillips curve analysis. According to this advanced expectations procedure economic agents will make use of all relevant and available information about the inflationary process in building up their inflation expectations, aiming at an improvement in the prediction of the inflation rate. Starting from this strong version of the rational-expectations hypothesis prediction errors can simply and solely arise from and be caused by random and unexpected monetary and real shocks in the economy. But naturally these expectational errors will result when the public has too little and incomplete information about all the factors determining the actual inflationary process. It is unlikely that such a situation will be continued, because in the course of time the public will ask for more information about the working of the economic system. When the economic agents behave rationally in Muth's sense they will soon encounter "surprise inflation" and will assimilate the inflow of new information in their expectations procedures. This means that the sources of mistakes and expectational-errors will be noted rapidly and will disappear systematically. Ultimately all the systematic and predictable determinants of the rate of inflation will become known and the individual expectations of economic agents will be unbiased forecasts consistent with this knowledge. Essentially rationality means that the current prediction error with respect to a variable is uncorrelated with past errors and other known information, for such correlations will already be perceived in the course of time and will be eliminated in the process of improving the predictions (Humphrey 1978, pp. 18–19).

In these circumstances the public's inflation expectations will always be equal to those generated by the actual inflationary process. As will later become apparent, the economy will then, according to Phelps, be in a continuous long-run equilibrium situation, unless there exists an unavoidable "surprise inflation" consequent on purely random real and monetary shocks in the economy (Humphrey 1976, pp. 14–15; Frisch 1977a).

5.2. Monetary policy implications of the rational-expectations hypothesis

Starting from the supposition that economic subjects are rational in building up their inflation expectations, based on all available relevant information about the actual inflationary process, inclusive of the systematic component of the monetary policy rules of the monetary authorities, the rational-expectations procedure together with the natural-rate hypothesis arrives at radical conclusions with regard to the effectiveness of monetary policy. Essentially the conclusion is that a systematic monetary policy is unable to generate production and employment effects either in the long or the short run. The authorities can only achieve real effects through organizing "surprising" and unforeseen monetary actions. However on the other hand such random and unexpected monetary impulses would substantially increase uncertainty with regard to economic policy, a situation which on balance will destabilize the economic system and inhibit economic activity.

The rather dramatic conclusion that even in the short run the trade-off between inflation and unemployment is a thing of the past (a vertical Phillips curve), is crucially dependent on the supposition that the public has a precise knowledge about the structure and the working of the economic process. Expectations will be adjusted immediately and without mistakes to the economic situation and to the information about planned economic policy measures. The economic subjects, as it were, have at their disposal perfect information regarding the impact of anti-cyclical policy measures and also have certain rational expectations about the time at which these measures will be taken. In this way the economy becomes immune to an economic stabilization policy and therefore orthodox counter-cyclical policy is foredoomed to failure (Willms 1977; Woll 1977).

The introduction of the rational-expectations hypothesis in macroeconomic theory essentially gives a strong theoretical foundation to Friedman's pessimistic view with regard to economic policy enacted in the sixties. This view can be summarized in short as follows. Because the policy makers are unable to make a precise prediction of economic development, they cannot succeed in reacting appropriately at the right moment and to the correct degree to mitigate fluctuations in economic activity. Therefore government intervention, a policy activism, will often produce pro-cyclical effects decreasing economic stability rather than increasing it (Sijben 1979).[2] Friedman points out that monetary authorities should abandon an active and anti-cyclical monetary policy. However they must be engaged in organizing and publicly announcing beforehand a fixed rate of monetary growth, such that there are no pushes from the monetary sector which could disturb the stability of the economy (monetary stability).

The strict rational-expectations hypothesis implies therefore that a systematic monetary policy, that is, a monetary policy based on feedback effects from the real sector of the economy, thus representing the reactions of policy makers to changes in the real variables, will not generate real effects even in the short run. This arises from the fact that according to this strong expectations mechanism economic agents already know beforehand the monetary policy pursued as well as its impact on the ultimate course of the economic process (transmission

---

2. See also in this context Chapter 2.

mechanism). They then incorporate this expected monetary policy behaviour in their economic decisions (wage and price-setting behaviour). So for instance the impact of an anti-cyclical money growth, induced by a fall in economic activity, will be expected by the economic subjects and incorporated in their inflation expectations and the concomitant economic decisions (Aftalion and Portrait 1978, p. 3; see also Ramser 1978a; Frazer 1978). As far as monetary authorities nevertheless like to influence production and employment positively they must organize a "surprise" inflation with the aid of an unpredictable monetary growth. Such growth arises suddenly and unexpectedly and will not be anticipated immediately beforehand in the economic decisions of the different market participants. However such a random monetary policy tactic becomes impossible when the public can fully predict the actions of monetary authorities.

Systematic (=expected) monetary policy actions consist of simple rules or reaction functions which relate economic policy variables to lagged values of other economic variables. These policy reaction functions can be estimated and then be incorporated in the prediction of the expected rate of inflation. In other words, rational economic agents are making use of their experiences with monetary behaviour of the authorities in the past (feedback information) to predict the future monetary policy actions. Ultimately on the basis of these predictions they make a correction beforehand with regard to the influence of the expected monetary policy behaviour on real variables by making the appropriate price and wage adjustments. In consequence stabilization measures, when they actually take place, will have no influence on the ultimate goals in the real sector because they have already been discounted in the economic decision-making process, thereby neutralizing the effectiveness of this policy activism. The only way in which economic policy can generate a short-run effect with regard to the real variables is to make monetary policy totally unpredictable. This means that in these circumstances monetary authorities will operate in a random and completely unreliable way or will change the policy reaction function secretly.

Apart from such monetary tactics, which essentially are not in accordance with the spirit of a correct implementation of the economic stabilization policy, rationalists are not able to suggest means through which policy makers might influence the real variables of the economic system. The authorities can only control a nominal variable, the rate of inflation say, and therefore they have to focus on that target insofar as they may wish to maintain a certain degree of monetary stability. This means that monetary policy has to be directed at fighting against inflation rather than at controlling real economic activity by mitigating the business cycle through policy activism. In this context therefore monetarists prefer the announcement beforehand of a fixed rate of monetary growth, based on the long-run development of real national income, to an anti-cyclical monetary policy. This situation in monetary policy, which would be without feedback effects from the real sector, leaves no scope for inflationary tendencies in the economy and can mitigate the destabilizing influence of inflationary expectations (Humphrey 1976, p. 19).

The above-mentioned views were recently expressed in unequivocal terms by Friedman as follows:

> it is a better approach to policy to say that you are going to cooperate with the people and inform them of what you are doing, so giving them a basis for their judgements, rather than trying to fool them. What the Sargent-Lucas argument and analysis really suggests is that you are fooling yourself if you think that you can fool them (1976, p. 232).[3]

Summarizing it can be concluded that the advocates of the rational-expectations hypothesis reject the concept of a trade-off

3. In this context see also Baily (1978), who applies the conception of rational expectations to the stabilizing potential of activist government fiscal policy. McCallum and Whitaker (1979) in a very recent article conclude that the systematic part of any feedback-rule for monetary *or* fiscal policy has no influence on the behavior of output relative to capacity, reinforcing the Lucas-Sargent-Wallace hypothesis. However "built-in stabilizers", making tax liabilities to respond automatically to current output levels, may influence the variability of output around capacity levels. These "built-in stabilizers" provide automatic and immediate adjustments to current disturbances and can therefore act to reduce the variability of output.

according to the original Phillips curve analysis in the long run as well as in the short run. In this respect there is a clear difference from the expectations-augmented Phillips curve according to the natural-rate hypothesis (adaptive expectations) as was presented in Chapter 4. According to the adaptive expectations with an irrational behaviour of economic agents, there is still some room left for a short-run trade-off because inflation expectations are not adjusted immediately to the change in the actual rate of inflation generated by monetary policy. So in these circumstances there is yet some scope for monetary authorities to organize a "surprise inflation" with the concomitant real effects during the period of transition to a macroeconomic equilibrium ($U_F = U_N$). However this result is out of the question within the rational-expectations framework, because the actual as well as the expected rate of inflation will adjust in the same way immediately to the expected and foreseen changes in monetary policy. In other words, according to the strong rational-expectations hypothesis, a systematic monetary policy, based on feedback effects from the ultimate goals in the real sector, can not achieve errors of prediction with respect to the rate of inflation and the concomitant short-run trade-off. In these circumstances policy activism or a Keynesian anti-cyclical monetary policy is foredoomed to failure. In such a case, with an expansive monetary policy, an upward movement along the vertical Phillips curve will take place (see Section 4.2), maintaining the macroeconomic equilibrium situation ($U_F = U_N$) but with a higher actual and expected rate of inflation ($\pi = \pi^*$). The difference between the short run and the long run is blurred, because in this case the effect that is considered under the natural unemployment rate hypothesis to be a purely long-run result after a learning process, now arises in the short run. The view that a determined monetary policy, a deterministic money supply rule, will have no influence on real economic variables in the long run equates with the well-known statement of the neutrality of money in (neo)-classical economics. Abstracting through a certain transition period to an equilibrium with rational expectations ("rational-expectations-equilibrium") implies an elimination of all the factors which make up the difference between the short run and the long run (Friedman 1979).[4]

The essential features of the theoretical views of the rationalists (Lucas-Sargent-Wallace) and the implications for monetary policy will be rendered and illustrated by a simple model in the next section.

5.3. A simple model under rational expectations

In order to interpret the advanced theory of rational expectations plainly, this section starts with a very simple model which points out the essential characteristics of that theory quite concisely.[5] The model consists of five equations, namely an expectations-augmented Phillips curve, an equation describing the actual inflationary process, a monetary-policy reaction function, and finally two equations rendering the conceptions of the rational-expectations procedure with regard to the rate of inflation and the rate of monetary growth. These equations show that because of the predictability of monetary policy the rational-expectations theory implies that no prediction errors can be organized and in consequence no short-run trade-off will arise. However an orthodox trade-off between inflation and unemployment always remains possible, but within the rational-expectations model this is only the result of unpredictable and random shocks from the real sector as well as from the monetary sector in the economy. For the rational-expectations hypothesis, in Muth's sense, gives predictions of the values of economic variables which can only differ from the ultimate corresponding model outcomes consequent on mistakes made by economic agents. These estimation errors are independent of the variables being used in generating the predictions. Therefore it is concluded that, assuming rational

4. See also Section 6.4.

5. The model is quoted from Humphrey (1978, pp. 14–22). The significance of rational expectations for the theory of economic policy can be found in Sargent and Wallace (1975, 1976); Barro (1976); Shiller (1978); Barro and Fischer (1976); Federal Reserve Bank of Minneapolis (1976); Lucas (1976); and Sargent (1973).

behaviour with regard to the forming of inflation expectations together with the natural unemployment rate hypothesis, a systematic trade-off between inflation and unemployment will disappear in the short run and in the long run. The accelerationist view, discussed in Chapter 4, according to which there exists a stable trade-off between the excess demand on the goods and labour markets on the one hand and the accelerated rate of inflation on the other hand also does not come into play within the rational-expectations framework. For when expectations are built up according to the inflation-generating process of the model, authorities are not able to deceive the public and put them on the wrong track by accelerating the rate of monetary growth to produce the concomitant acceleration of the inflation rate.

Following Humphrey, in the remainder of this section the equations of the model mentioned above will be rendered and explained successively.

The expectations-augmented Phillips curve equation

$$\pi - \pi^* = \gamma(U_N - U_F), \quad \gamma > 0 \qquad (1)$$

This equation, a variant of Friedman's natural unemployment rate hypothesis, represents a trade-off between an unexpected rate of inflation and the rate of unemployment, rendered by the disequilibrium situation on the goods market and on the labour market ($X = U_N - U_F$) and where the price expectations coefficient α is assumed to be equal to one (see Section 4.2). In recent economic literature concerning the rational-expectations theory this equation is often considered as a macroeconomic supply relationship (Sargent and Wallace 1975).[6] This equation is based on the view that entrepreneurs produce at "normal" capacity when the actual rate of inflation equals the expected

6. The aggregate supply is homogeneous of degree zero with respect to actual and expected prices. This supply relationship can be formulated as follows: $y_F = y_N + \beta(\pi - \pi^*)$, $\beta > 0$, where y_F represents the actual production and y_N the production level in accordance with the natural rate of unemployment (U_N). In this context see also Lucas's view in Section 4.2.

rate of inflation and that the rate of utilization of capacity would increase should a "surprise inflation" be organized ($\pi > \pi^*$ and $U_F < U_N$).[7] As is explained in detail in Section 4.2, the Lucas supply-mechanism implies the following. The individual entrepreneurs will interpret an initial unexpected excess demand on the goods market, consequent on an expansive monetary policy, as a particular increase in demand relevant to their own market position and not as a general increase in demand with a concomitant general rise of the price level. They think that their relative market position has "improved" and consider the price increase as being relative, a factor which induces them to increase production. Whatever the interpretation may be, prediction errors generate production and employment effects resulting in a deviation of actual production from "normal" production, with concomitant changes in the rate of capacity utilization (trade cycle). This deviation disappears as soon as the prediction errors with respect to the expected rate of inflation are corrected ($\pi = \pi^*$, $X = 0$ and $U_F = U_N$), and the macroeconomic equilibrium, according to Phelps, will be restored.

The inflation-generating process

The following equation is essentially a dynamic formulation of the cash balance theory of the Cambridge School and expresses the inflation-generating process of the model.

$$\pi = m + \varepsilon \tag{2}$$

The actual rate of inflation is equal to the algebraic sum of the adjusted rate of monetary growth (m) and a stochastic disturbance term (ε), which is assumed to have an expected value of zero. This adjusted rate of monetary growth (m) is simply the algebraic difference between the rate of growth of money supply and the rate of growth of real production whereby the latter variable is an approximation of the trend rate of growth of

7. The concept of "normal" production capacity corresponds with the monetarist idea of the natural unemployment rate (U_N).

the real demand for money. The disturbance term ε indicates that the rate of inflation can also be influenced by temporary disturbances which originate from the supply side of the economy. In this context the unexpected large increases in oil prices brought about by OPEC-countries in 1974 is the example most used in the literature (Gordon 1978, p. 338).

The equation above implies that a change in the rate of the nominal money supply will result in an equal change in the rate of growth of nominal income in the same direction. This reasoning also applies to a change in the adjusted rate of monetary growth (m) and the rate of change of the price level (π), so that inflation can be considered purely as a monetary phenomenon. The relationship above can be interpreted as an expression of a crude monetarist view of the transmission process, according to which monetary impulses act upon national income directly through aggregate expenditures (direct mechanism).

The anti-cyclical monetary growth rule

The third equation of the model is a monetary policy reaction function, describing how the monetary authorities will react to changes in the level of economic activity. It refers to an anti-cyclical money growth rule, through which the development of the rate of monetary growth will be dependent on the actual development of the ultimate targets of economic policy in the real sector. In this way monetary policy behaviour is endogenous to the economic model. This relationship can be rendered as follows:

$$m = \psi(U_{N-1} - U_{F-1}) + \mu, \quad \psi' < 0 \tag{3}$$

The actual rate of monetary growth is dependent on the excess demands on the goods market and on the labour market in the previous period ($U_{N-1} \neq U_{F-1}$) and on a stochastic disturbance term (μ), which has an expected value of zero. The interpretation of this policy reaction function runs as follows. The responsible monetary authorities, using the anti-cyclical money growth rule, try to correct the excess demand situation on the goods and labour market in the preceding period by adjusting the rate of monetary growth in the current period. This essentially means that the central bank will pursue a tightening monetary policy when there is an upswing in economic activity and will aim at a cheap money policy when there is a relative fall in economic activity ("leaning-against-the-wind"). This policy reaction of the monetary authorities concerns the systematic part of the anti-cyclical money growth rule.

The equation above also demonstrates that a perfect and complete control of the rate of monetary growth cannot be achieved by using this monetary feedback rule. The uncontrolled part of the actual rate of money growth is rendered by the stochastic disturbance term (μ), which is the non-systematic, unpredictable, component in the monetary supply. This disturbance term causes an unexpected deviation of the rate of monetary growth from the monetary policy strategy aimed at by monetary authorities. However this term can also refer to an intentional monetary tactic, consciously organized by the monetary authorities – "a surprise inflation" (Gordon 1976b, p. 200).

The expected rate of inflation

The price expectations function describes the construction of rational expectations with respect to the rate of inflation. According to Muth's conception rational inflationary expectations will be in accordance with the predictions generated by the current inflationary process (see equation (2)). Since this equation indicates that the actual rate of inflation equals the sum of the current adjusted rate of monetary growth and a disturbance term, it now holds that the expected rate of inflation, predicted by this equation, equals the sum of the expected monetary growth rate and the expected value of the disturbance term concerned. As this last expected value is assumed to be equal to zero, the rational-expectations hypothesis proposes that the expected rate of inflation agrees with the expected rate of monetary growth (m^*). Algebraically this can be described as follows:

$$\pi^* = m^* \qquad (4)$$

These symbols represent the public's rational expectations of the rate of inflation and of money growth (adjusted) and also express the mathematical expectations – the latter indicating the expected values of the stochastic variables, in this case the rate of inflation and the monetary growth rate, calculated from a model that in principle renders a precise description of the actual inflationary process. This is the nucleus of the proposition that the public's inflation expectations are built up rationally, in Muth's sense, when they agree with those implied by the relevant economic model. In the economic literature it is often pointed out in this context that the expected rate of inflation can be expressed formally as the mathematical expectations of the actual rate of inflation, conditional on all relevant information available at the moment when the expectation was formed. This can be reflected symbolically as follows:

$$\pi^* = E(\pi \mid I),$$

where E represents the mathematical expectation and I is the known information set at the moment when the inflation expectations were built up. Since this information includes the actual inflationary mechanism according to equation (2), it follows that the expected rate of inflation will be equal to the mathematical expectation of the inflationary process concerned, i.e. to the sum of the expected values of the rate of monetary growth, m^*, and of the stochastic disturbance term. ($\varepsilon^* = 0$) (Humphrey 1978, p. 20, footnote; Mullineaux 1977a, p. 16).

The expected rate of monetary growth

Finally the conceptions of the rational expectations hypothesis are also used to determine the expected rate of monetary growth (m^*). In this context the rational expectation with respect to the rate of money growth agrees with the prediction of the mechanism generating the actual rate of money growth (the anti-cyclical monetary growth rule of equation (3)). Economic subjects make use of their observations about monetary policy behaviour in the present as well as in the past and build up their expectations about the systematic component of the monetary growth rate accordingly. Prediction of the future development of monetary policy will only be possible when the public could have been able to observe the reactions of monetary authorities to different economic situations during a rather long period or when the money growth rule has previously been publicly announced.

This means that within the rational-expectations framework the expected value of the anti-cyclical monetary growth rule determines the expected rate of monetary growth. Since the monetary policy reaction function (3) has a systematic (predictable) component, whose expected value is equal to it, and also contains a non-systematic component (a stochastic disturbance term) with an expected value of zero ($\mu^* = 0$), the expected rate of monetary growth can be rendered as follows:

$$m^* = \psi(U_{N-1} - U_{F-1}) \tag{5}$$

In other words, the expected rate of monetary growth is determined by the predictable and systematic component of the known anti-cyclical money growth rule. This means that economic subjects have a complete knowledge of monetary policy behaviour, except insofar as the disturbance term is concerned. They will make use of all this knowledge in building up their expectations with respect to the monetary growth rate (see Barro 1977a).

By substituting equations (2) to (5) into equation (1), the rational expectations model can be confined to the following reduced-form equation:

$$\mu + \varepsilon = \gamma(U_N - U_F) \tag{6}$$

from which a Phillips curve relation results:

$$U_N - U_F = \frac{\mu + \varepsilon}{\gamma} \tag{7}$$

This reduced-form equation implies that the orthodox trade-off according to the conception of the Phillips curve can only come about insofar as there exists a "surprise inflation" caused by random and unforeseen real (ε) and monetary (μ) shocks in the economy. Further, from equation (7), it can be deduced that the systematic component of the monetary growth equation (3) has disappeared, which means that a systematic monetary policy (an anti-cyclical money growth rule) can no longer achieve real effects. Because of the supposed rational-expectations procedure, even in the short run monetary authorities will not succeed in organizing "surprise inflation" systematically. Every systematic monetary policy rule with feedback effects from the ultimate goals in the real sector, incorporated with all the past information, becomes a part of the information available at the beginning of the prediction period and will therefore be taken into account in constructing the expected rate of inflation (see equations (4) and (5)). Only an unexpected rate of monetary growth (μ) causing an unforeseen change in the rate of inflation will be able to influence the economic policy targets in the real sector of the economy. In the appendix the operation of the rational-expectations model is elucidated with the aid of some simple numerical examples.

The above-mentioned view means that the makers of monetary policy can only influence the real variables of the economic system in two ways. First of all they can pursue a "random" monetary policy, through which the rate of monetary growth changes in a completely random and unpredictable way. This essentially means that the central bank manipulates the non-systematic component (μ) in the monetary policy reaction function unpredictably. Next it is also possible for the authorities to change the anti-cyclical monetary growth rule secretly. In these circumstances production and employment will be influenced during a transition period, when the economic agents are deceived and will have to learn the monetary policy behaviour gradually (Friedman 1979). However it is unlikely that such monetary policy behaviour will achieve lasting real effects. For rational economic subjects, in gathering information, will also learn to predict changes in monetary policy rules in the same way as they have learned to predict the systematic anti-cyclical monetary growth rule. In this context Shiller remarks:

> After a policy is adopted it may at first be difficult for individuals to make forecasts of future economic variables and they must rely on crude

> guesses. . . . The essential assumption that rational expectations theorists then make, however, is that after a transition period, the economy will converge on a dynamic path for which the expectations mechanisms which are involved in determining the path are indeed rational. The economy will have reached what we will here call a "rational expectations equilibrium" (Shiller 1978, pp. 3–4; see also Sargent and Wallace 1976, p. 181).

All in all what is implied is that only random monetary policy tactics can influence real economic activity. However it is difficult to consider these monetary accidents as a sound basis for an active economic stabilization policy of the government.

Summarizing it can be stated that the strong version of the rational-expectations hypothesis implies that only errors of prediction with regard to the expected rate of inflation can cause a deviation from Phelps's concept of the macroeconomic equilibrium situation ($U_F \neq U_N$), and that these errors are only short-lived and arise by chance. Therefore a systematic monetary policy rule will have no impact on the real economic variables because this behaviour rule will already be incorporated completely in the economic decision-making processes. This means that the expected money growth, through the impact on the expected rate of inflation, will find expression in wage and price increases and not in changes in production and employment (Barro 1977a; Mullineaux 1977a, pp. 16–25). Apart from unpredictable, real or monetary shocks, there will always exist a macroeconomic equilibrium, and systematic monetary movements will not cause disappointed expectations or transition influences with respect to real economic activity.

A possible trade-off is a completely random phenomenon which cannot be regulated by systematic monetary policy behaviour. Therefore there is no longer any room left for an anti-cyclical macroeconomic stabilization policy. Economic policy activism will only affect the rate of inflation, which will adjust immediately to the expected change in the rate of monetary growth consequent on the publicly known anti-cyclical monetary growth rule. The full impact of the expected monetary policy actions ultimately manifests itself in an equal change of the actual and the expected rate of inflation.

In consequence, according to the rationalists, monetary

authorities have to concentrate on monetary stability, maintaining the purchasing power of money, because there is no room left to mitigate fluctuations in real economic activity through an activism in monetary policy (an anti-cyclical money growth rule). Korteweg concludes in this context,

> Automatization in monetary policy, expressed by a fixed money growth rule without feedback effects is an optimal strategy, when the public behaves rationally in the sense that only unforeseen changes in the monetary instrument condition its real behaviour and that expectations with respect to economic variables are not consistently worse than the predictions of the economic model relevant to the variables concerned (Korteweg 1976a, p. 502, my translation; see also Federal Reserve Bank of Minneapolis 1977; Parkin 1975).

Although the rational-expectations theory is an attack on Keynesian stabilization policy, it is also to a certain degree an attack on the monetary policy views of the monetarists. For this expectations mechanism flies in the face of the monetary conceptions of, for instance, Friedman, where he points out that an increase in the money supply will first be expressed in a change of the real component of national income and after some time in a price rise. The available and distributed impact of monetary impulses on the quantity and price components of national income is, according to Lucas, essentially a reflection of changes in the expectations structure of economic agents with respect to the significance and influence of monetary policy. Since it is not possible at any moment to indicate with certainty what are the precise expectations of the public, monetarists cannot predict the influence of monetary impulses on the economic process, especially with respect to the quantity and price components of national income (*Business Week* 1976).

6. A critical review of the rational-expectations theory

In the preceding exposition, the discussion has focused in detail upon the consequences of an introduction of the rational-expectations hypothesis for the effectiveness of monetary policy in a macroeconomic model, incorporating an anti-cyclical money growth rule and an expectations-augmented Phillips curve, or in other words a macroeconomic supply relation with the natural unemployment rate hypothesis. In concluding our theoretical reflections it is important to trace the benefits and disadvantages connected with the theoretical views of the rationalists.

6.1. Rational versus irrational behaviour

An important advantage of the introduction of the rational-expectations mechanism to macroeconomic theory arises from the fact that the construction of inflation expectations, made endogenous to the model, occurs as a part of the optimal behaviour of economic agents (Humphrey 1978, pp. 21–22). In this way the theory of price expectations becomes more in accordance with the other parts of economic analysis. So for example the theory of consumers' and producers' behaviour assumes that economic agents behave as rational calculating individuals, aiming at an optimization with respect to their consumption and production decision-making processes, to looking for new jobs (job-searching processes on the labour market), to capital decision-making, and so on. In this respect the rational-expectations theory is preferable to other competing explanations about the formation of expectations, where the public exhibits rather irrational behaviour resulting in systematically biased forecasts (see Section 4.3). The adaptive expectations-generating mechanism makes use of one or other rule of thumb independent of the stochastic characteristics of the time path of the economic variable of which expectations have to be formed. In contrast the rational-expectations hypothesis is the only expectations procedure denying that economic agents will make expectational errors consistently in the course of time. In this context it has to be noticed that this by no means implies that the public has "perfect foresight" or that predictions are always precise. Rather the rationalists emphasize that the public will discover a certain regularity in the prediction errors and then eliminate these in an appropriate way. Economic agents, as it were, get on the track of the actual inflation-generating process and make use of this information in building up inflation expectations. Since the rational-expectations theory assumes that these inflation expectations correspond with the mean value of the actual inflationary process, these predictions will, on average, have no bias. As far as there still arise expectational errors, these will have a random characteristic and not a systematic feature. This is not true for the other, competing, expectations procedures, which generate expectations on the basis of irrational schemes and which are consistently wrong.

These irrational expectations hypotheses are difficult to justify in a theoretical respect because systematic prediction errors can be explained less easily than rational behaviour. A theory assuming that economic agents will not make errors continuously appears intuitively more acceptable than theories implying the opposite. Friedman points out in this context: "'Rationality' is a word with mostly favorable *a priori* connotations. No one readily thinks of his own actions as irrational, and few economists are comfortable with the idea of modeling irrational behavior" (1979, p. 32).

Assuming that some benefits arise in improving the predictions it is difficult to maintain that systematic errors and the concomitant wrong and costly economic decisions will be continued. There will always be economic agents, observing the mistakes, who are stimulated to correct them and make profits chargeable to those who omit the adjustments. Others will perceive this behaviour and receive incentive to make the appropriate corrections – so the profit motive and the competition will reduce the prediction errors to purely random phenomena.

6.2. Rationality and macroeconomic models

Next the theory of rational expectations has an important consequence for the theory of economic policy, because the assumed rational behaviour of the public results in a change of the parameters of the econometric models when there is a change in economic policy. The traditional approach with regard to a quantitative evaluation of alternative economic policy measures makes use of an estimated macroeconometric model and then examines the behaviour of the endogenous variables at alternative future values of the policy variables (exogenous variables). Sometimes it is possible to do calculations directly with the help of a reduced-form equation, while in other cases the numerical values of the endogenous variable can be obtained by simulations. Lucas and Wallace in particular have criticized this approach and have pointed out that the structure of the economic model is sensitive to changes in economic policy behaviour. Lucas notes, "any change in policy will systematically alter the structure of econometric models" (1976, p. 41; see also Andersen 1979; Mishkin 1978). The authors posit that simulations with models, assuming fixed parameters, produce wrong and deceiving results because those simulations do not take account of the fact that public behaviour (including their expectations with respect to the values of economic variables) is crucially dependent on the economic policy implemented. The aforementioned authors point out that every economic policy measure will cause a change in the behavioural parameters so that the stability of the economic structure becomes unsettled. This means that economic models assuming constant values of the parameters cannot be used in evaluating alternative economic policy measures because the behavioural parameters must be considered endogenous variables because of changing public behaviour. This arises from the fact that the behavioural equations in the economic models have been deduced from the individual optimal decision rules of the economic agents. These rules themselves are also partly based on the expectations of economic subjects with respect to the development of relevant economic variables (Lucas 1976; see also Gordon 1976a; Sargent and Wallace 1976, pp. 179–180; Wallace 1976). For in contrast to the traditional theory of economic policy, postulating a mechanical extrapolation of a model with constant values of the parameters, the public in fact does not react as mechanically as the econometrically-determined behaviour equations imply. Economic agents, interested in economic policy, will watch the policy behaviour of monetary authorities carefully and try to discover the real resoluteness and thoroughness with which the makers of monetary policy implement their announced intentions.

The reaction of the public to an economic policy decision is critically dependent on the way this policy is implemented. As far as monetary policy is discretionary and so does not follow a fixed pattern, policy behaviour will become known to the public only gradually. It is possible even that the public will gain no insight at all into this behaviour. The influence of monetary policy behaviour on the economic behaviour of the public will have an unsystematic and erratic course, making it very difficult to predict in the context of economic policy decision processes. However when an economic policy measure, for instance a fixed money growth rule, is publicly announced and discussed beforehand, then it will be possible to predict the resulting changes in the structure of the model on the basis of past experiences. This means that the behaviour of economic agents as well as their expectations must be involved in preparing and implementing economic policy measures more closely than was the case until recently. Lucas notices in this context:

> More particularly I shall argue that the features which lead to success in short-term forecasting are unrelated to quantitative policy evaluations, that the major econometric models are (well) designed to perform the former task only, and that simulations using these models can, in principle, provide *no*

> useful information as to the actual consequences of alternative economic policies (1976, p. 20; see also Wallis 1977, pp. 37–43).[1]

In the traditional forecasting models an unchanged basic structure of the model is implicitly assumed, while in practice however this structure changes according to the phase of the business cycle. Changes in economic policy will alter this structure systematically and will also alter the behavioural relationship (optimal decision rules of the economic agents) on which the structure is based. Frazer expresses these views concisely when he states:

> The decision making may be a continuous process and learning related to the decision may take place as new information is obtained. Sampling (data, new information) may be from a changing universe as it goes on continuously. . . . This learning from data and experience contrasts with the role of classical probability in least-squares regression analysis. The former suggests a world where sampling in the statistical sense may be from a changing universe and the latter depends on the assumption of an *unchanging universe*. Changes in expectations about future events and outcomes are impounded in the parameters ("structure") of least-square estimated structural relations (1978, pp. 349–350).

The preceding reflections essentially mean that using constant behavioural parameters in macroeconometric models implicitly assumes that economic agents do not adjust their expectations procedures, even when they imply biased forecasts. So these models show disequilibrium situations which can be avoided by taking into account the fact that the individual economic subjects have learned to make their economic decisions dependent also on expected economic policy behaviour (rational behaviour). Wallace expresses this view as follows:

> Macro-econometric models consist of estimated relationships behind each of which, at best, is an implicit partial equilibrium model of some aspect of the behavior of some sector of the economy. These models are meant to provide invariance arguments, but ironically, a close look at any of them provides a noninvariance argument. These noninvariance argu-

1. Here again Walters remarks "Consistent expectations pose an interesting methodological problem. If economic research does establish the efficacy of the quantity theory, then such research itself will generate a theory of expectations that will *change* the parameters of the system" (1971, p. 281).

ments point out the permanent disequilibria implicit in macro-econometric models; and they also point out that the extents of such disequilibria are made dependent on the policy regime in effect since no offsetting response of the public is allowed (Wallace 1976, pp. 89–90).

Although many economists recognize that the rationalists (Lucas, Sargent and Wallace, among others) have made an important contribution to macroeconomic theorizing by pointing out that the significance and the forming of (inflation) expectations cannot be omitted with impunity, recent macroeconomic literature contains some fundamental criticisms of the rational-expectations theory. These critical remarks, especially referring to the assumptions of the rationalists, will be presented in the following four sections.

6.3. Information costs and information availability

A first point of criticism pertains to the crucial assumption of the rational-expectations theory implying that economic agents have at their disposal all the relevant information and make use of this efficiently in building up their inflation expectations. Friedman points out that in macroeconomic models with rational expectations the way in which economic subjects gather and interpret the information and knowledge about the working of the economic model in aiming at formulating expectations which correspond to actual outcomes of the relevant economic theory is not exactly made clear. In this context he makes a distinction between, on the one hand, an efficient utilization of the available information, and information availability itself on the other hand (Friedman 1979, p. 25; see also Gordon 1977).

With regard to the utilization of information, which, according to Muth, is an essential part of the rational-expectations hypothesis, in general the following can be noticed. Starting from an optimalization behaviour of economic subjects it will be rational economically to utilize the available relevant information up to the point where the marginal benefits of gathering information (to enable a more precise prediction to be made) equal the marginal costs connected with the intended activities. This means that as far as marginal costs are positive not all the available information will be used. In contrast in his publication Muth implicitly assumed that the information concerned could be acquired and interpreted without cost, for he assumes that the information is fully incorporated in the rational forecasts. However rational behaviour in Muth's sense is naturally not costless and the costs connected with the gathering and interpretation of information will in practice put the brakes on the use of the factors of production in these prediction activities. Therefore there exists, as it were, a trade-off between the benefits and costs connected with the gathering and interpretation of additional information (see Feige and Pearce 1976; Darby 1976).

In a recent elucidated paper Cukierman introduces more generality into the information structure of rational expectations models. His modification of the multi markets rational expectations models of the type discussed by Lucas and Barro refers to the following. Individuals in any market may sample currently more prices than just the current price on their *own* market reducing temporary confusions between aggregate and relative price movements. Next economic agents choose the amount of their current information so as to minimize the sum of the costs of getting information and of being off their full information demand and supply curves. The balancing of these costs and the benefits to be reaped from more information determines the structure of information in the economy. The optimal amount of information is derived as the amount which minimizes the sum of the costs of information collection and the costs of being off full information output (see Cukierman 1979). In this way the amount of information collection effort is allowed to be determined endogeneously. Cukierman then concludes that under those circumstances any change in the variance of aggregate excess demand shocks (whether caused by real or monetary elements) affects the equilibrium level of information in the economy. The more wide spread is current price information, the nearer will equilibrium prices and outputs be to their full information counterparts, reinforcing the Lucas hypothesis on the effects of monetary variance on output-behaviour.

The second, most controversial, point of criticism expressed by Friedman refers to the specific supposition of the rationalists that the relevant information available at the time of prediction is sufficient to make an optimal forecast of the value of the economic variable concerned. This strong supposition essentially means that economic agents act "as if" they have full knowledge of the structure of the economic process which ultimately determines the actual value of the variable in question. This means that one needs to know not only the specification of the equations of the model and the relating different arguments, but also the coefficients of the model, such as the income and interest elasticity of the demand for money, the (real) interest elasticity of investment demand, and so on. For according to Muth expectations are built up by a reduced-form equation with respect to the exogenous variables, generating the actual outcome of the variable to be predicted. This special information requirement is described by Friedman as follows:

> ... the information availability assumption of rational expectations hypothesis is that economic agents not only know the relevant current and past observations, plus the future values of selected time series, but also have whatever additional knowledge is required to transform this information into *objectively* unbiased conditional expectations of the time series to be predicted (Friedman 1979, pp. 26–27).

Further it must be noticed that the individual economic agents each use a different, but in their view correct theoretical economic model, in building up expectations with regard to the economic variable concerned. Every individual economic subject acts rationally with respect to his specific model. This means that the various economic agents can attach a quite different significance to the same information set about the economic process, resulting in a divergence between the expectations and the concomitant decisions of the various economic subjects. However the question still remains regarding which is the "correct" model of the economy and how the economic agents gather and interpret all the necessary knowledge to make an optimal inflation forecast.

6.4. Semi-rational expectations hypothesis

After having presented a detailed exposition of the assumptions of rationalists with regard to information costs and information availability, Friedman concludes in his theoretically high-level publication that there is essentially talk of a learning process in the rational-expectations theory, which is consistent with the spirit of the rational-expectations hypothesis as originally put forward by Muth. He considers the supposition of the availability of information as a substitute for the well-known proposition that in the long run all relevant adjustment processes will be achieved, culminating in a long-run equilibrium situation in the economy. This is pointed out as follows:

> In particular, the information availability assumption included in the rational expectations hypothesis implies the completion of a convergence process which imparts to the associated analysis the character of long run equilibrium (Friedman 1979, p. 32; DeCanio 1979).

In these circumstances the rational-expectations hypothesis closely links up in an analytical sense with the adaptive expectations mechanism as was explained in Section 4.3. In the long run a continuation of gathering information and knowledge will become no longer relevant and the (neo) classical conclusion of the neutrality of money in the economy will arise. This means in essence that some time elapses before the public gathers the information and knowledge about the precise working of the economic model. The public then adapts its behaviour to this model, aiming at formulating the rational inflation expectations as was intended by Muth. So Friedman, in his theoretical reflections, concludes that as far as the strong assumption with regard to full information availability and to the costless gathering and interpreting of information is not realistic, the formation of inflation expectations in the short run will occur through a so-called "optimal learning procedure". This expectations procedure corresponds greatly with the aforementioned adaptive expectations mechanism, whereby there is in reality some room left for an effective macroeconomic stabilization policy during the transition period to a long-run equilibrium situation. The optimal learning procedure has a rather hybrid character because it refers, as it were, to a combination of the features of the rational-expectations hypothesis on the one hand and of the adaptive expectations theory on the other hand. The element of the rational-expectations hypothesis involved is the impact of a change in the rate of monetary growth in the long run, while the element of the learning process is a reflection of the uncertainty with regard to the precise process of adjustment to the new long-run equilibrium situation.

With this *semi-rational expectations hypothesis* one can distinguish between the initial change of the expected rate of inflation, based on public knowledge about the ultimate effect of the original monetary impulse in the long run, and the change of inflation expectations in the medium term during the transition period. This last change or revision and adaptation of the inflation expectations is positively related to the difference between the long-run equilibrium value of the rate of inflation and the actual rate – a feedback effect consequent on a learning process (Mathieson 1977, pp. 551–554; see also Frenkel 1975; Mussa 1975). The semi-rational expectations structure is based on the hypothesis that the market participants have an estimation of the long run effects resulting from a change in monetary policy, but they are uncertain with regard to the adjustment process from the initial equilibrium to the new long-run equilibrium situation. This semi-rational expectations mechanism or optimal learning procedure of the economic subjects could be described, as an analogy of the adaptive expectations theory, as a simple weighted average of the naive, mechanical, adaptive expectations and the advanced rational expectations.

Taylor (1975), subscribing to the views of Friedman and McCallum, points out in this context that the public is accumulating monetary experiences during the transition period ("learning period") to rational expectations and so he speaks about "transitional expectations". Insofar as economic agents will in the course of time combine the inflow of new information about the economic process with past information and consequently gradually adjust their inflationary expectations, then monetary policy will still be able to exert a systematic influence on the real economic variables. In other words monetary policy will recover a part of its effectiveness which was completely lost in the strong version of the rational-expectations hypothesis. However it must be noticed that it is not out of the question that such a transition period will be continued, so that a rational-expectations equilibrium will not be achieved. This situation might occur when the monetary authorities prefer to maintain superior information with respect to the public, fully exploiting this advantage and passing little or no information to the economic agents (see Section 6.6). Apart from an explicit short-run learning process in the rational-expectations theory there naturally remains room only for a descripton of long-run equilibrium situations. Therefore in essence the importance of an economic stabilization policy vanishes. Although such an optimal learning procedure or semi-rational expectations hypothesis is consistent with the spirit of Muth's rational-expectations theory, this expectations mechanism is not really in accordance with the purely applied definition of the rational-expectations hypothesis because irrational behaviour can actually exist during a rather long "learning period".[2]

6.5. Long-term contracts and expectations theory

A second point of criticism pertains to the basic assumption in the theoretical model of the rationalists about the perfect flexibility of nominal wages and prices, even in the short run, as far as the expected, that is, the publicly announced, changes in the rate of monetary growth are concerned. This essentially implies that the Walrasian tâtonnement process is always in operation (the auction market), where at any moment transactions will only take place at equilibrium prices. The theory of rational expectations is fundamentally based on a free market economy and the relative-price mechanism, in which stability in the private sector stands central. Therefore a stabilization policy

2. In this context McCallum (1976) speaks about "partly rational expectations". See also Gordon (1977, pp. 130–131).

by the government aiming at a regulation of the business cycle is ruled out beforehand, for prices are perfectly flexible in the auction market; they smooth out market disequilibria quickly and market participants make the decisions on the basis of known demand and supply functions. The information about the market situation is assumed to be gathered without cost. The reasoning of the rationalists proceeds as follows. When the economic agents build up their inflation expectations rationally, every expected rate of monetary growth will be immediately and completely transformed into a correspondent increase of the nominal wage and price level, eliminating any real effects on economic activity.

In economic literature much attention is given to the fact that in practice it may take a rather long period to clear the markets (Gordon 1976b; Poole 1976; Okun 1975). In this context Gordon remarks:

> Very recently there have been signs that research resources are beginning to shift from model-building exercises in which output changes are caused by price "surprises" to those which attempt to explain price and wage contracts, and hence sluggish price adjustment, as the result of micro economic optimizing behaviour (Gordon 1976b, p. 207; see also Modigliani 1977).

The basic view of these wage and price contracts stems from the fact that in an uncertain economic world economic agents can achieve a profit by entering implicitly or explicitly into a contract. These contracts need not refer only to labour relations and goods transactions, but also to any spread of risks connected with uncertain events in the future.

So Okun distinguishes between "auction markets" on the one hand, whereby prices clear the markets immediately, and "customer markets" on the other hand, characterized by sticky prices because of current contracts, resulting in the market-clearing process coming about through, for instance, forced quantity adjustments. The contracting view is based on the following reasoning. In the "customer's market" substantial information costs (time, effort, and so on) are entailed in comparing the different purchase alternatives, stimulating the buyer to contract continuously with the customary supplier, whose supply has turned out satisfactory in the past. However the buyers should be able to put confidence in unchanged terms of delivery, because otherwise they will leave the regular suppliers to start costly search activities on the markets. The supplier in his turn derives benefit from stable prices to keep his customers. Since higher prices will stimulate buyers to buy elsewhere because this implies a relative fall in marginal information costs, suppliers do not react or react only sluggishly with their prices when the demand changes in the short run. This essentially means that the supplier implicitly agrees to keep a stable price in exchange for an implicit promise by the customers to continue the clientship. Such implicit contracts will only work well when the parties concerned adhere to certain rules of the game. The entrepreneur-supplier in his turn will not immediately adjust his price to the short-run demand and supply relations, aiming at discouraging the buyers from starting search processes on the market. Moreover frequent price changes mostly involve high costs (price-lists, announcements, and so on) and it is often very difficult to judge whether a given change in demand is of a temporary or a more general character (see Section 4.2). In these circumstances profit-maximization behaviour in the long run may very well result in non-optimization behaviour in the short run.

This contract view also comes into the picture on the labour market where there exists an explicit or an implicit wage contract.

Azariadis (1973), Baily (1974) and Gordon (1974) attempt to give an explanation of the sluggish adjustment of wages to changed economic conditions by using the contract theory. They assume that long-term wage contracts essentially are prompted by a different view of employers and employees with regard to uncertain future incomes. These authors postulate that employers are risk-neutral in this respect or act as risk-takers while employees can rather be considered as risk-averters. The entrepreneurs, aiming at a minimization of wage income according to their profit-maximization behaviour, hire employees and sell them simultaneously an "insurance" against fluctuations in their incomes. The employees in their turn transmit the risk of a possible income loss to the risk-neutral employer in exchange for a fixed nominal or real income. Therefore employers as well as employees like to fix wage contracts for a certain period. At the beginning of the contract period wages and prices are fixed at a level which is assumed to be consistent with an equilibrium on the goods market during the coming period. However when, during the contracting period, notwithstanding the cause, the actual demand curve diverges from the demand curve expected at the time the contract was settled, resulting in a disturbance of the equilibrium in the real sector, a new price-wage configuration will be required to restore the equilibrium. In these circumstances quantity adjustments (shorter working hours, overtime, and so on) will take place in the real sector during the contracting period instead of the direct appropriate wage and price adjustments. The lag in the wage and price adjustments caused by the supposed implicit or explicit contracting period of course has consequences for the conclusions with regard to the effectiveness of economic stabilization policy, especially monetary policy. As far as monetary authorities are able to influence the macroeconomic aggregate demand within the contracting period, it will be considered as an unexpected demand-pull which cannot be taken into account in fixing up the wage contract, so therefore real effects can be generated. However since the makers of monetary policy are not committed to such contracts, they can react very quickly to unexpected economic events and in this way they still have the opportunity to stabilize economic activity to some extent (see also Hall, 1975; Phelps 1977; Ramser 1978b).

It can be said that insofar as wages and prices are fixed during a certain period, a change in the rate of monetary growth during the contracting period can in fact achieve real effects. In these circumstances monetary authorities still have some room in executing an active, anti-cyclical monetary policy, for long-term contracts mean that economic agents are not able to incorporate new information about the actual economic situation immediately, although this may thoroughly change their future economic outlook. All this means that the orthodox ideas with regard to curbing unemployment need not be abandoned simply and solely because the public builds up inflation expectations rationally. If the flexibility of wages and prices is restricted in the short run, it is less important whether expectations are formed rationally or not. For in these circumstances one critical condition about the neutrality of money is no longer fulfilled. The length of the contracting period concerned is very important in this view and in all probability will be dependent on the strength and the duration of the demand shifts. The better an anti-cyclical policy will be able to eliminate the undesired effects of sudden and unforeseen demand shifts and therefore will be more effective, the longer the contracting period may be, but this increases the need for further anti-cyclical measures (Arak 1977a, pp. 18–19; Poole 1976, pp. 502–503). Fischer has shown that overlapping long-term wage contracts offer the possibility to pursue a monetary stabilization policy, although inflationary expectations are built up rationally. He constructs a model with rational expectations and long-term nominal (non-indexed) wage contracts, involving a Keynesian-like element of a temporary wage stickiness. This arises from the fact that monetary authorities can change monetary policy more frequently than the negotiators can change their wage contracts. For during the contracting period monetary authorities can react to the new inflow of information about recent disturbances of the economic process through their monetary policy actions, providing a stabilizing role for an active monetary policy even when that monetary policy behaviour is fully anticipated by the public. The effectiveness of monetary policy is no longer dependent on organizing a "surprise inflation" or on deceiving the economic agents. It is true that with these long-term contracts monetary policy behaviour is fully anticipated, but since the actual policy will also be based on information which becomes available during the contracting period it can affect the short-run behaviour of real output. Fischer (1977a, p. 203) points out: "Monetary policy loses its effectiveness only if long-term contracts are indexed in an elaborate way that duplicates the effects of single-period contracts" (see also McCallum 1977; Phelps and Taylor 1977).[3] Barro criticizes the conclusions of the theoretical explanations of Fischer, Phelps and Taylor which assert that the nominal wage contracts in a rational-expectations model leave some room for an active monetary policy during the contracting period (Barro 1977b; Fischer 1977b). Barro's criticism has a normative character and refers especially to the form and the content of the wage contracts. He points out that the authors mentioned above assume that in the contracting approach only the nominal wage is determined. The demand for labour by the entrepreneur is determined with the aid of a given demand curve for labour, dependent on the real wage rate, which itself is negatively related to the general price level. According to Barro this contracting approach is applied only to one aspect of the contract, that is, the nominal wage determination, while the other aspect of the labour market, the supply of labour, or the employment determination (trade-off: working versus leisure) is entirely omitted. He considers such contracts to be sub-optimal since no negotiations take place about the quantity component of the wage contract, namely the amount of employment. An unexpected increase in the rate of monetary growth, according to the Fischer contract, will give rise to a fall in the real wage rate, consequent on the generated price rise, and will ultimately result in a positive output and employment effect. In this context it can be noticed that when the actual amount of employment is determined according to the rule: $l = \min(l^d, l^s)$, a fall in the real wage rate caused by the generated price rise will not result in an increase of employment. For starting from the initial labour market equilibrium:

$$l^* = l^s\left(\frac{\bar{W}}{P_0}\right) = l^d\left(\frac{\bar{W}}{P_0}\right),$$

3. In a very recent publication McCallum (1978) has established the basic compatibility of sluggish price adjustments and the Lucas-Sargent proposition, that policy makers cannot exploit the output-inflation trade-off in any useful fashion.

a fall in the real wage rate will result in an increase in the amount of employment of the order of:

$$l = l^s\left(\frac{\bar{W}}{P_1}\right) < l^*$$

where $P_1 > P_0$.

Formulated in terms of the standard graph of the labour market, Barro apparently ascribes to Fischer the assumption according to which there is talk of a fully elastic supply of labour ($l = l^d$) at a real wage rate below the equilibrium level $(\bar{W}/P_0)^*$. However Barro speaks about an optimal contractual arrangement, according to the spirit of Pareto welfare economics, where the amount of employment arranged in the wage contract is equal to the amount arising when the labour market is cleared with perfect wage and price flexibility. The author clearly aims at the Walrasian tâtonnement-process, whereby the contracting partners, in this case the auctioneer, make one integrated decision about the price and the quantity simultaneously. At any other employment level the marginal product of labour for the employer will depart from the marginal value of time for the employee. In these circumstances both contracting parties would be better off revising the contracts continually, resulting ultimately in the optimal situation according to Pareto ($l = l^*$). So besides the nominal wage rate Barro's contracts incorporate an employment rule ($l = l^*$), through which the quantity variable does not react to monetary disturbances because the equilibrium real wage rate, contractually arranged, will remain the same. In these circumstances there is no room left for a counter-cyclical monetary policy to affect short-run output behaviour.

However although Barro's analysis is theoretically very elegant, it must be judged as less realistic especially because a continuous revision of such complicated contracts involves substantial costs. For in practice a nominal wage rate is contractually arranged whereby the entrepreneur determines the amount of production and labour input. Where the contracts are indexed the nominal wage rate will be adjusted to changes in the general price level but not to other unforeseen events.

6.6. The meaning of superior information

A third point of criticism in the economic literature pertains to the strong assumption that the private economic agents possess exactly the same information with respect to the actual inflationary process as the makers of monetary policy. Following Korteweg I feel it is more realistic to assume that the public does not have full access to the relevant economic model and to the required information about the operation of the economic process to make forecasts with the model concerned. The monetary authorities' superior information with respect to the public might manifest itself in the following two ways. On the one hand there exists the possibility that the authorities deliberately do not transmit the required information to the public, while on the other hand it may occur that centralization of gathering and interpreting of information gives rise to economies of scale, so that in this respect the authorities gain an advantage over the decentralization of the information activities of the individual economic subjects (Korteweg 1976a, p. 502). In both cases monetary authorities will be able to realize real effects in the short run through an active monetary policy, because in these circumstances not every monetary action will be foreseen, so the public can be systematically deceived. In his theoretical explanations about the importance of the relative information position between the monetary authorities on the one side and the private market participants on the other side, Barro states:

> when the monetary authority has superior information about the economy, the provision of the information to the public is an alternative to an active stabilization policy. An argument for the superiority of stabilization policy would have to be based on the costs of transmitting and using the relevant information (1976, pp. 23–24; see also Barro and Fischer 1976, p. 162; Taylor 1975, p. 1020, Woglom 1979).

From this quotation it appears that a more efficient arrangement of the supply of information in the economy can result in a more rational formation of inflation expectations by the economic agents. In this respect a plea for a publicly announced intended rate of monetary growth is more realistic. Moreover factors of production previously used in the process of information production can then be set free to be employed in the production of goods, so that a net social gain arises along these lines. However insofar as monetary authorities prefer to maintain superior information there will be more room left for a counter-cyclical monetary policy. This monetary policy activism can only be justified on account of arguments in the sphere of the provision of information insofar as, on the one hand, monetary authorities gain an information advantage through "economies of scale", and, on the other hand, it is very costly to transmit the economic information to the economic agents for their interpretation. In this context Howitt remarks:

> in an informationally decentralized economic system with set-up costs of information acquisition it will clearly be worthwhile for the monetary authority to use information that private agents choose to ignore. . . . Since no private agent has a direct concern for the aggregate state of the economy, he will not find it worthwhile to consider many of the aggregate variables that could profitably be considered by the monetary authority who is directly concerned with such aggregates (1977, pp. 3–4).

However deliberately keeping back economic information must be considered less acceptable in a democratic society and is rather difficult to reconcile with the intention of an accurate and consistent implementation of economic policy. Barro points out that in a democratic environment economic policy actions must be based on the preferences of the citizens and notices: "In my model, there appears to be no basis for policy deception as long as the policymaker's objective is based on minimizing the gap between actual and full information output" (1976, p. 24).[4] Therefore such an objective cannot mean that the makers of monetary policy are desirous of deceiving the economic subjects and stimulating them to take sub-optimal decisions. Moreover in the highly-developed Western economies it has grown into a custom that economic information (predictions about interest rates, exchange rates, rates of inflation, balance of payments,

---

4. In this context Lucas also remarks "You can't run a democratic society by trickery" (Gazzard 1978, p. 74).

and so on) is publicly disseminated very quickly. And so sources of information for the public are broadened, and the public is able to build up rationally its expectations about economic variables to a greater extent (Cukierman 1979, p. 225).

7. Summary and conclusions

From the preceding theoretical reflections it may be deduced that as far as monetary authorities aim at a prediction of the rate of inflation and at curbing this inflation it is necessary to get a better insight into the mechanisms generating inflationary expectations. Until recently empirical researchers always started from adaptive or auto-regressive models in their attempts to specify the expectations mechanism, while very recently the theory of rational expectations was given consideration. As is pointed out in the preceding chapters, the adaptive or auto-regressive models assume that inflationary expectations are generated on the basis of past observed rates of inflation. However the rational-expectations hypothesis is that the public's inflation expectations are equal to the mathematical expected value of the rate of inflation. The expectations of the economic agents are based on a full knowledge about the operation of the actual inflationary process and also on a complete availability of all the relevant information about the economic model (equations of the model and the parameter values).

Although within the framework of the behaviour theory the adaptive expectations procedure might be considered rather naive, it still has the advantage of being better workable in an empirical respect. However rational-expectations models are theoretically very elegant and attractive, because they link up with the economic paradigms of rational behaviour in an economic world with negligible information costs and full certainty (auction models).

Starting from the criticisms with regard to the rational-expectations hypothesis, as these were presented in Chapter 6, in our opinion a more eclectic view, namely the weak version of the rational-expectations theory, as put forward by Friedman, is preferable, for this so-called "optimal learning procedure" or semi-rational expectations mechanism has a more realistic character on the one hand and is in accordance with the spirit of Muth's rational-expectations framework on the other hand. According to this expectations procedure economic agents, in building up their inflationary expectations, initially use past observed inflation rates as a basis whereupon gathering and interpreting of information can take place almost without cost. From this foundation they will gradually build up inflationary expectations more rationally according to a growing knowledge of the operation of the economic process and of monetary policy behaviour in the course of time. The inflow of new information about the economic process will be used to adapt and improve the expectations based on the original learning model of adaptive expectations. After a time-consuming learning process this procedure converges to a long-run equilibrium or a "rational-expectations equilibrium". During this transition period some importance can still be attributed to a macroeconomic stabilization policy. Therefore it may be concluded that as far as in practice there is talk about a learning process, about the existence in an institutional respect of long-term contracts with some rigidity of wages and prices, about positive information costs and superior information by monetary authorities, it will still be possible to mitigate fluctuations in economic activity by using an active monetary policy.

The critical remarks put forward in the economic literature may have explained that the rational-expectation theory cannot be considered as a representative interpretation of the actual behaviour of the economic subjects. Notwithstanding the learning processes which have taken place the impact of countercyclical measures on short-run output behaviour will be continued. However one should have no illusions about the elimination of structural disequilibria in the economy through an expansive monetary or fiscal policy. The economic policy consequences which the advocates of the rational-expectations theory draw from their refined macroeconomic models are acceptable to a certain extent. So maintaining a fixed rate of monetary growth and a trend-rate of growth of government expenditures will undoubtedly contribute to a stabilization of inflationary expectations which will ultimately benefit the stability of the total economy. We cannot fully endorse the strong version of the rationalists which implies that the introduction of rational expectations in macroeconomics has completely removed the basis for an economic stabilization policy, so that the end of the era of the active counter-cyclical policy has come about. This liberal-orthodox view however is not new, and is put forward regularly, sometimes with other arguments, when there exists a certain dissatisfaction with regard to the practical economic policy. In practice there is almost always an unstable economic development which compels the authorities to a certain intervention in the economic process. After all it cannot be denied that notwithstanding the short-run-oriented stabilization policy of the sixties, since the early seventies the Western economies have been confronted with a fall in the rate of economic growth, a rise in the rate of unemployment, an accelerated rate of inflation, and a strengthening of the business cycle. Consequently a widespread scepticism has arisen with regard to the effectiveness of post-Keynesian economic stabilization policy. However this policy should be oriented to the long run, focusing on a stabilization of *inflation expectations*. Within this framework a fixed rate of monetary growth should be preferred to a discretionary monetary policy, for a discretionary monetary policy with feedback effects of the ultimate targets in the real sector will be anticipated in the course of time, both with regard to the time of implementation and its impact on the economic process. Policy activism of this nature would therefore lose its effectiveness in mitigating fluctuations in economic activity.

A monetary policy strategy consistent with the views which comprise the rational-expectations hypothesis is a policy emphasizing the curbing of inflation. In this context what must be considered is a public preannouncement of a fixed monetary growth rule, whereby a certain (low) target with regard to the rate of inflation is aimed at. In this way it will be possible to achieve a greater predictability and stability of monetary growth, which undoubtedly will give rise to a stabilization of inflation expectations. In consequence prediction errors with the concomitant wrong economic decisions may disappear. In that perspective we hold the view that a gradual reduction and stabilization of the monetary growth rate in accordance with the long-term rate of growth of real production may provide an essential contribution to curbing inflation and to a stabilization of inflation expectations. For the sake of good order it must be noticed that our analysis refers to the implications of the expectations structure for monetary policy in a closed economy. Such a supposition may be justified for a country like the United States, where the economy bears a rather closed character, so that the rate of monetary growth can better be controlled than in a country like the Netherlands where the influence of the international economic relations on the money supply is substantial (De Nederlandsche Bank 1978, p. 20).[1] The permanent and increasing inflation of recent years in the Western world is caused in essence by a continuous and even an accelerating growth of the money supply in relation to the growth of real production. The inflationary process is essentially a monetary phenomenon which cannot be brought about unless the monetary authorities provide the required "monetary fuel" (apart from a possible rise in the velocity of circulation). It is obvious that decreasing the growth rate of the money supply must not be a sharp and abrupt switch in the short run, because there still remains an existing rate of inflation, so that a too rapid and sharp policy adjustment, with the associated "surprise-element" ($\pi < \pi^*$) might cause a liquidity squeeze with harmful results for production and employment. A policy of gradually reducing the monetary growth rate commensurately with the real growth

1. The president of the Dutch central bank states that the restrictive money policy behaviour in 1978, aimed at reducing the liquidity ratio in the national economy, has undoubtedly contributed to a mitigation of the inflation rate and the concomitant inflationary expectations in the Netherlands (De Nederlandsche Bank 1978, p. 21).

rate of the economy may contribute to the elimination of the destabilizing impact of inflationary expectations. Wage negotiations and price setting by firms should not be determined (1) by the rate of inflation in the recent past, but rather by (2) the lower rate of inflation which will be allowed by the monetary authorities in the near future. A monetary policy in this sense of (1) is based on a policy rule of conduct with feedback effects from the real sector (an anti-cyclical monetary growth rule). In these circumstances the economic behaviour of individuals is irrational, with their inflationary expectations being derived from the past observed inflation rates. However (2) relates to a monetary policy without feedback effects from observed economic variables (a preannounced monetary growth target). In this context Duwendag points out:

> All market participants are given a monetary framework in advance (monetary budget) and thereby set some psychological data for the price and wage policy of the unions and the entrepreneurs, shifting the responsibility for inflationary price increases (1977, pp. 2–4).

The fixed monetary growth rule, which must be maintained consistently, will not generate harmful real effects because the impact of this monetary policy rule on the price level will be incorporated in the price expectations of the public, excluding in this way a "surprise inflation". The monetary authorities have to maintain the policy of controlled monetary growth to convince the public that they are actually determined to banish the inflation not only temporary but permanently. This means that the central goals of monetary policy must involve an elimination or a reduction of the uncertainty of the public with regard to the future development of the price level, thus restoring confidence in the future (investment activity). Such a guideline for monetary policy can break the wage-price spiral by revising the inflation expectations downwards, resulting in sound and more stable monetary relations in the long run. Korteweg puts this concisely as follows:

> To achieve this monetary rule current growth rates of money should be gradually reduced to their target values. A stable and preannounced monetary growth rate would help to prevent inflation, would prevent

> inflationary expectations from being mistaken, would restore the information context of money and prices, would make the monetary authorities predictable and the future less uncertain (1977, p. 5).[2]

Although it cannot be denied that the forces from the sphere of the income distribution threatening the purchasing power of money are very strong, we still judge it be possible to mitigate these forces by a preannouncement of a gradual reduction of the monetary growth rate without causing an abrupt and serious contractive disturbance of the real economic process. In determining policy variables, rational expectations are formed by learning the rules that the controlling agencies are following. In this context Parkin puts it pointedly:

> However, it is necessary to forecast actions, not stated intentions; therefore, until enough evidence is available to convince the people that the monetary authority is in fact going to act in accordance with its stated intention, there will be ample scope for forecasting errors (1977, p. 229).

It is obvious that an essential supplement of this monetary growth rule should be an income policy according to which real wages are increased in correspondence with the long-term growth rate of labour productivity. Very recently the abovementioned views were in essence also expressed by Zijlstra, president of the Dutch central bank, where he states

> There is no doubt that the publication of fixed monetary targets can make a contribution to *tempering* the inflationary climate, especially by influencing expectations. . . . To be successful, such a policy must be adequately supported by developments in the two other policy areas that I have mentioned (i.e. wage and price policy and fiscal policy). With all this in mind, it need hardly be argued, at least in my view, that a central bank should be an *independent* body with a statute which clearly states its task of maintaining the value of money (1979, p. 13).

At the end of his lucid article Zijlstra notes that the total money supply must be considered one of the most important macro-economic policy instruments and that the basic philosophy of a central banker should be that an excessive money supply will sooner or later lead to inflation, to the debasement of money.

---

2. Special attention should be given to Korteweg's empirical study (1978).

However we are of the opinion that all this can only be realized if all the participants in the economic process are prepared to cooperate, and if less authority and responsibility is given to organized groups than has been the case with many Western countries in the recent past.

Finally it can be noticed that the rational-expectations theory, which has been explained in detail in the monetary-theoretical literature since the early seventies, is a provocative challenge to advocates of a monetary policy activism. There are many indications that point out that the discussions with regard to the different expectations mechanisms and their consequences for macroeconomic stabilization policy, especially with respect to monetary policy, will still be further intensified.

Appendix

The purpose of this appendix is to elucidate the operation of the rational-expectations model with the aid of some simple numerical examples. The model will then be extended to express the stagflation phenomenon whereby the effects of alternative monetary policy rules will be illustrated. It will appear very clearly that the character of monetary policy behaviour is not relevant for the development of the real variables in the economy, because systematic monetary impulses cannot organize a "surprise inflation". As is known from the foregoing theoretical analysis only the unexpected impulses, generating prediction errors, will bring about real effects in the economy.

The calculations are based on the following simple rational-expectations model, explained in Section 5.3.

The macroeconomic aggregate supply-function

$$y_F = y_N + \beta(\pi - \pi^*), \quad \beta > 0 \tag{1a}$$

Making use of Okun's Law, this equation can be transformed into the *expectations-augmented Phillips curve relationship*

$$\pi - \pi^* = \gamma(U_N - U_F), \quad \gamma > 0 \tag{1b}$$

The actual rate of inflation

$$\pi = m + \varepsilon \tag{2}$$

The anti-cyclical monetary growth rule

$$m = \psi(U_{N-1} - U_{F-1}) + \mu, \quad \psi < 0 \tag{3}$$

The expected rate of inflation

$$\pi^* = m^* \tag{4}$$

The expected rate of monetary growth

$$m^* = \psi(U_{N-1} - U_{F-1}) \tag{5}$$

Substitution of equations (2) to (5) into equations (1a) and (1b) renders the following reduced-form equation of the model:

$$y_F - y_N = \beta(\varepsilon + \mu) \tag{6a}$$

or

$$U_N - U_F = \frac{\varepsilon + \mu}{\gamma} \tag{6b}$$

From these equations Okun's Law can be represented as follows:

$$U_N - U_F = \frac{1}{\beta\gamma}(y_F - y_N) \tag{6c}$$

The operation of the model

For simplicity a stationary economy is assumed in which the level of natural unemployment and output remains constant. A change of the rate of inflation (π) or of the monetary growth rate (m) in this model is in accordance with a demand shift (see Gordon 1976b, p. 187). This can be explained with the aid of Figure 2. An unexpected impulse, expressed by a positive change in the values of ε or μ, generates a demand shift (D′D′), given the supply curve (SS), resulting in an equilibrium situation at point B with a higher price level (P_1) and a greater amount of output (Q_1). As was described in Section 4.2, the individual entrepreneur confronted with an unexpected (non-systematic) rise in total monetary demand will interpret the changed market situation as a random increase in the demand for his own product at current prices. The uncertainty with regard to the changed market situation means that there results a demand-induced price rise and an output effect manifested along the given supply curve (SS). This also means a shift along the given

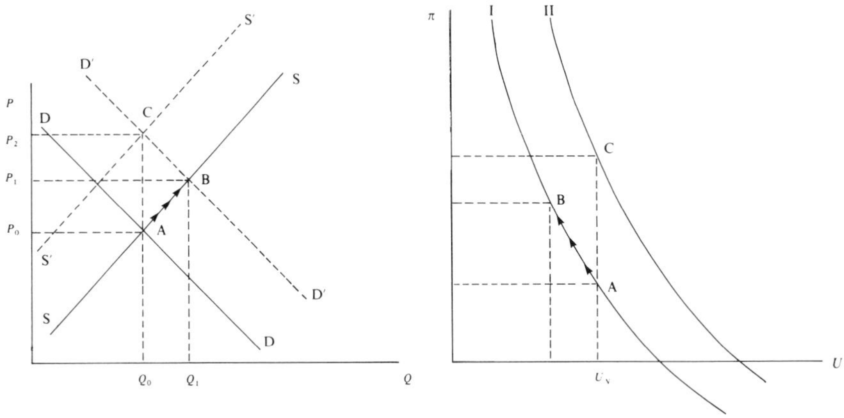

Figure 2.

Phillips curve I (AB). However when the entrepreneurs perceive that the changed market situation was not specific to them they adjust their behaviour, shifting the supply curve to the left. When the initial demand shift is fully anticipated, so that entrepreneurs are not deceived by the price rise, the supply curve will shift immediately to the left (S′S′) and the concomitant Phillips curve to the right (II), resulting in a new equilibrium with the initial quantity of goods demanded and supplied (point C), but with a higher price level (P_2). An anti-cyclical monetary policy behaviour will slightly confuse this picture. When the monetary authorities react counter-cyclically on an unexpected impulse by a change in monetary growth, the demand curve shifts in an opposite direction and might be shifted back to the original position when the monetary reaction is precise enough. In that case the supply curve remains unchanged, because the monetary policy reaction is fully anticipated by the firms.

However when the makers of monetary policy do not react precisely with a change in the rate of monetary growth, then the supply curve shifts in such a way that the initial "natural" level of output will be reached at a higher or a lower price level.

When there are no impulses at all in our stationary economy, the assumed equilibrium values of the strategic economic variables, maintained continuously, are as follows:

$$\pi = \pi^* = 0;$$
$$m = m^* = 0;$$
$$y_F = y_N = 100;$$
$$U_F = U_N = 5;$$
$$M = 100;$$
$$P = 1.0.$$

The values of the coefficients β and γ are assumed to be equal to 1 and 5 respectively, while the reaction coefficient ψ in the anti-cyclical monetary growth rule takes the value -5.

First of all it is assumed that in period $t = 1$ an unrepeated unexpected disturbance arises in the inflationary process, represented by the value $\varepsilon = +10$. Then the following schedule results:[1]

	π	π^*	y_F	y_N	U_F	U_N	m	m^*	M	P
$t = 0$	0	0	100	100	5	5	0	0	100	1.0
$t = 1$	+10	0	110	100	3	5	0	0	100	1.1
$t = 2$	−10	−10	100	100	5	5	−10	−10	90	1.0
$t = 3$	0	0	100	100	5	5	0	0	90	1.0

Starting from the equilibrium situation $t = 0$, the impulse in period $t = 1$ generates a "surprise inflation" so that the actual rate of inflation deviates upwards from the expected rate of inflation. According to the Lucas supply mechanism this results in a downward deviation of the actual unemployment level from its natural level, while the actual production level exceeds the natural level. However monetary authorities only react with a monetary restriction in the second period, and this is fully anticipated by the economic agents and is appropriately incorporated in their decisions. According to the suppositions of the rational-expectations theory, the expected monetary growth

1. For simplicity in the numerical examples second and higher-order effects are ignored.

rate and so the actual and the expected rate of inflation will be adjusted directly and simultaneously in a downward direction. Ultimately a new equilibrium situation ($t = 3$) arises with no real effects as compared with the initial equilibrium situation ($t = 0$), but on balance there exists a reduced money supply at an unchanged price level. When the monetary policy is tightened (or eased) in the second period, the equilibrium value of the price level becomes lower (or higher) in comparison to the initial situation, without causing any real effects in the economy. This means that an anti-cyclical monetary growth rule within the framework of the rational-expectations theory has consequences only with regard to the rate of inflation, and not with respect to production and unemployment. This arises from the fact that economic agents have a perfect insight into the reactions of the makers of monetary policy.
The influences of an unrepeated non-systematic monetary impulse, represented by the value $\mu = +10$ in period $t = 1$, can be scheduled as follows:

	π	π^*	y_F	y_N	U_F	U_N	m	m^*	M	P
$t = 0$	0	0	100	100	5	5	0	0	100	1.0
$t = 1$	+10	0	110	100	3	5	+10	0	110	1.1
$t = 2$	−10	−10	100	100	5	5	−10	−10	100	1.0
$t = 3$	0	0	100	100	5	5	0	0	100	1.0

The unexpected random shock in the monetary sector generates a "surprise inflation" in the first period, resulting in the usual positive real effects. In the next period ($t = 2$) monetary authorities react with a tightening of monetary policy and, owing to the chosen value of the reaction parameter, $\psi = -5$, the unexpected impulse is exactly compensated, resulting in the same money supply and price level as in the starting situation ($t = 0$). Economic agents fully anticipate this monetary reaction and take it into account in their economic decisions. Neither the strength of the monetary reaction nor the fact that authorities will react at all will have any real effects when monetary policy is fully expected by the public. Monetary policy actions will only influence the *nominal* values of economic variables without changing the operation of the real economic process.

An extension of the model

In the two preceding numerical examples the influence of unexpected impulses, generating "surprise" inflation with its concomitant short-run output effects, were analysed. In both cases the random disturbances refer to the demand side of the economy. However to analyse the impulses arising from the supply side a third disturbance term, ρ, with an expected value of zero, has to be introduced, modifying the aggregate supply function as follows.

$$y_F = y_N + \beta(\pi - \pi^*) + \rho \tag{1a'}$$

Then the expectations-augmented Phillips curve can be rendered as follows:

$$\pi - \pi^* = \gamma(U_N - U_F) + \rho' \quad \rho' = \frac{-\rho}{\beta} \tag{1b'}$$

Taking these equations into account the modified reduced-form equations of the model can be written as:

$$y_F - y_N = \beta(\varepsilon + \mu) + \rho \tag{6a'}$$

and

$$U_N - U_F = \frac{\varepsilon + \mu - \rho'}{\gamma} \tag{6b'}$$

The influence of a positive supply shock, represented by the value $\rho = +10$ in period $t = 1$, can be scheduled as follows:

	π	π^*	y_F	y_N	U_F	U_N	m	m^*	M	P
$t = 0$	0	0	100	100	5	5	0	0	100	1.0
$t = 1$	0	0	110	100	3	5	0	0	100	1.0
$t = 2$	−10	−10	100	100	5	5	−10	−10	90	0.9
$t = 3$	0	0	100	100	5	5	0	0	90	0.9

The unexpected impulse from the supply-side of the economy generates positive real effects in the same period ($t = 1$), so that actual production and unemployment deviate from the natural level of these economic variables. This happens without a deviation in the actual rate of inflation from the expected rate, and so without a "surprise inflation" and, according to Lucas, the concomitant operation of the supply mechanism. In the next period monetary authorities react with a monetary contraction, as will be expected by the economic subjects, ultimately resulting in a fall in the money supply and in the price level. Eventually on balance output and unemployment will be stabilized at the initial natural level. It may be concluded that also in this case monetary policy reactions merely influence the *nominal* values of the economic variables, but the real variables remain unchanged.

The stagflation phenomenon

Stagflation can be defined as the economic situation characterized by the coexistence of depression and inflation, a simultaneous price rise and fall in production, with increasing unemployment. This phenomenon cannot be explained by the orthodox Phillips curve analysis and the concomitant Keynesian demand management policies. Stagflation still remains the most baffling economic problem of the seventies, a problem which, because of unwanted side effects, will not respond satisfactorily to traditional remedies, whether classical or Keynesian. What is novel in the present economic position, in some countries at least, is the persistence of inflation when the depressing influences have become operative. As was analysed in the foregoing chapters the accelerationists' theory could explain the coexistence of a high inflation rate and a high rate of unemployment, but not the coexistence of increasing unemployment and an accelerated rate of inflation.

If we assume that the stagflation phenomenon in the Western industrialized countries initially arose from the cost-push influence of the oil price increase, considered as an unrepeated, non-systematic, and unexpected impulse, then this phenomenon can be elucidated by the simple rational-expectations model in the following way.[2] The oil price increase must be interpreted in

2. It is obvious that the increase in oil prices of the early seventies involves a structural change in the Western economy, especially with regard to the natural rate of unemployment and of production.

the model as a positive value of the error term in the inflationary process, $\varepsilon = +10$, and a negative supply shock, $\rho = -30$. The influences of these unrepeated, non-systematic, impulses in period $t = 1$ can be scheduled as follows:

	π	π^*	y_F	y_N	U_F	U_N	m	m^*	M	P
$t = 0$	0	0	100	100	5	5	0	0	100	1.0
$t = 1$	+10	0	80	100	9	5	0	0	100	1.1
$t = 2$	+20	+20	100	100	5	5	+20	+20	120	1.3
$t = 3$	0	0	100	100	5	5	0	0	120	1.3

The numerical example points out that in the first period the disturbances generate a price rise and a contraction of output, so that actual unemployment diverges upwards from its natural level. The general price level has risen due to a contraction in the real sector of the economy. In the second period monetary authorities react by an expansion of the money supply. According to the rational-expectations hypothesis this monetary policy behaviour is fully anticipated by the public, resulting in a simultaneous rise of the actual and the expected rate of inflation, as well as the actual and the expected rate of monetary growth. Owing to the fact that there is no "surprise inflation" in the third period, production and unemployment will return to the natural level but at a higher money supply and a higher price level.

Alternative monetary policy rules

It is interesting to analyse what the consequences of alternative monetary policy strategies within the rational-expectations framework would be. Up to now it has always been assumed that monetary authorities implement an anti-cyclical monetary growth rule induced only by the given development of the real variables in the economy, while a change in the price level does not induce monetary actions at all. The following alternative monetary policy rules will now come up for discussion.

A. An anti-cyclical monetary growth rule, also financing the inflationary process;
B. An accommodating or passive monetary policy induced by the development of nominal national income;

C. A fixed monetary growth rule, irrespective of the development of the real variables or the price level.

A. When the monetary authorities implement an anti-cyclical monetary policy with feedback effects from the real variables as well as inflation financing, equations (3) and (5) of the model have to be modified as follows:[3]

$$m = \psi_1(U_{N-1} - U_{F-1}) + \psi_2\pi_{-1} + \mu, \quad \psi_1 < 0, \psi_2 > 0 \quad (3')$$

$$m^* = \psi_1(U_{N-1} - U_{F-1}) + \psi_2\pi_{-1} \quad (5')$$

Assuming the following values of the monetary reaction parameter $\psi_1 = -5$, of the disturbance terms, $\varepsilon = +10$ and $\rho = -30$, the undermentioned schedule results:

	π	π^*	y_F	y_N	U_F	U_N	m	m^*	M	P
$t = 0$	0	0	100	100	5	5	0	0	100	1.0
$t = 1$	+10	0	80	100	9	5	0	0	100	1.1
$t = 2$	+30	+30	100	100	5	5	+30	+30	130	1.4
$t = 3$	+30	+30	100	100	5	5	+30	+30	160	1.7

According to this monetary policy behaviour, fully financing the unavoidable inflation with a lag of one period, a continuous inflation which is fully anticipated by the economic subjects results, so the effects upon the real variables fail to come about. Monetary authorities inflate national income but are not able to organize a "surprise" inflation, with its concomitant influence on real production and employment. It appears that in this case the money supply, the general price level, the actual and expected rate of inflation, and the actual and expected monetary growth rate, are higher than when monetary policy reacts only to the development of the real variables.

B. Assuming that monetary authorities use the development of actual nominal national income as an indicator of their policy behaviour (a passive monetary policy), then equations (3) and (5) have to be modified as follows:

3. ψ_1 represents the reaction of monetary policy authorities to the development of real variables; ψ_2 represents this reaction to the development of the inflation rate, and for simplicity it is assumed to be equal to 1.

$$m = \psi(\dot{y}_{-1} + \pi_{-1}) + \mu_1 \quad \psi > 0 \tag{3''}$$

$$m^* = \psi(\dot{y}_{-1} + \pi_{-1}) \tag{5''}$$

Starting from the values $\psi = +1$, $\varepsilon = +10$ and $\rho = -30$ the following schedule results:

	π	π^*	y_F	y_N	U_F	U_N	m	m^*	M	P
$t = 0$	0	0	100	100	5	5	0	0	100	1.0
$t = 1$	+10	0	80	100	9	5	0	0	100	1.1
$t = 2$	−10	−10	100	100	5	5	−10	−10	90	1.0
$t = 3$	+10	+10	100	100	5	5	+10	+10	100	1.1
$t = 4$	+10	+10	100	100	5	5	+10	+10	110	1.2

Because of the decrease in nominal income (the supply shock dominates the price shock) resulting from the initial unexpected shocks, monetary authorities react with a tightening of monetary policy ($t = 2$) so that the price level falls. In the second period however nominal income increases, resulting in an expansion of the money supply in the third period. However this monetary reaction just involves a continuous inflation, fully anticipated by the economic subjects, with no consequences for the real variables in the economy. Of course it is conceivable that the price rise dominates the contraction of the real variables, resulting in an increase of nominal income in the first period. This can be analysed by assuming the values $\varepsilon = +20$ and $\rho = -30$, generating the following schedule:

	π	π^*	y_F	y_N	U_F	U_N	m	m^*	M	P
$t = 0$	0	0	100	100	5	5	0	0	100	1.0
$t = 1$	+20	0	90	100	7	5	0	0	100	1.2
$t = 2$	+10	+10	100	100	5	5	+10	+10	110	1.3
$t = 3$	+20	+20	100	100	5	5	+20	+20	130	1.5
$t = 4$	+20	+20	100	100	5	5	+20	+20	150	1.7

In this case there arises a continuous fully-anticipated inflation in the second period, which is fully incorporated in the economic decisions so that there are no real effects upon the economy.

C. When monetary policy behaviour involves a fixed, pre-announced, monetary growth rate, equations (3) and (5) have to be modified in the following way.

$$m = m_0 + \mu \tag{3'''}$$

$$m^* = m_0 \tag{5'''}$$

Starting from a fixed monetary growth rate according to the rate of growth of real production, including the unavoidable inflation in the transition period, the following schedule results, given $\varepsilon = +10$ and $\rho = -30$:

	π	π^*	y_F	y_N	U_F	U_N	m	m^*	M	P
$t = 0$	0	0	100	100	5	5	0	0	100	1.0
$t = 1$	+10	0	80	100	9	5	0	0	100	1.1
$t = 2$	0	0	100	100	5	5	0	0	100	1.1
$t = 3$	0	0	100	100	5	5	0	0	100	1.1

In this case it is assumed that the power of the makers of monetary policy is so strong that they pay no attention to the development of the real economic process. Within the rational-expectations framework this policy behaviour will be appropriate, because monetary authorities cannot influence production and unemployment. The counter-cyclical monetary policy only generates price movements with no effects on short-run output behaviour.

Changing monetary policy behaviour

A change in monetary policy behaviour can be related to a change of the reaction parameter (ψ) as well as to a transition to another policy rule. Here we analyse the case where the monetary authorities switch from a counter-cyclical monetary policy with inflation financing to a fixed monetary growth rule without a public preannouncement. This means that policy-makers secretly change the monetary policy strategy. According to the strong variant of the rational-expectations hypothesis economic agents will immediately adjust to this new policy rule so that it is only during one period that a "surprise inflation" emerges.

Starting from the values of the error terms $\varepsilon = +10$ and $\rho = -30$ and an actual monetary policy behaviour according to equation (3‴), economic agents expect an anti-cyclical monetary growth rule according to the equation:

$$m^* = \psi_1(U_{N-1} - U_{F-1}) + \psi_2\pi_{-1}, \quad \psi_1 = -5, \psi_2 = +1 \quad (5')$$

However it appears during the second period that the actual policy behaviour is in accordance with equation (3‴), so economic subjects are deceived during this period. They then adjust their expectations appropriately according to the equation:

$$m^* = m_0 \quad (5''')$$

so that the following schedule results:

	π	π^*	y_F	y_N	U_F	U_N	m	m^*	M	P
$t = 0$	0	0	100	100	5	5	0	0	100	1.0
$t = 1$	+10	0	80	100	9	5	0	0	100	1.1
$t = 2$	0	+30	70	100	11	5	0	+30	100	1.1
$t = 3$	0	0	100	100	5	5	0	0	100	1.1

In the second period economic subjects expect a rate of money growth of 30 per cent, generating also an expected rate of inflation of the same amount. However the actual rate of inflation appears to be equal to zero, resulting in a negative "surprise inflation", with its concomitant substantial effects for the real economic variables of the system. This results from the fact that economic decision-making processes are based on a higher expected rate of inflation, which is not authorized by the monetary authorities involving a liquidity squeeze. In the third period economic agents' expectations adjust to the new lower actual rate of growth of money, so the actual rate of inflation will be equal to the new expected rate of inflation. Output and employment then return to the natural level.

Bibliography

T. Aftalion and R. Portrait, Propositions pour un stratégie monetaire. *Banque*, January 1978.

L. Andersen, Selection of a monetary aggregate for economic stabilization. *Federal Reserve Bank of St. Louis Review*, October 1975, pp. 9–15.

L. Andersen and J. Jordan, The monetary base – explanations and analytical use. *Federal Reserve Bank of St. Louis Review*, August 1968a.

L. Andersen and J. Jordan, Monetary and fiscal actions: a test of their relative importance in economic stabilization. *Federal Reserve Bank of St. Louis Review*, November 1968b.

P. Anderson, Rational expectations forecasts from non-rational models. *Journal of Monetary Economics*, January 1979, pp. 67–80.

M. Aoki and M. Canzoneri, Reduced forms of rational expectations models. *The Quarterly Journal of Economics*, February 1979, pp. 59–71.

M. Arak, Rational expectations: a survey of the evidence and implications. Research paper, Federal Reserve Bank of New York, March 1977a.

M. Arak, Some international evidence on output-inflation trade-offs: comment. *American Economic Review*, September 1977b, pp. 728–731.

C. Azariadis, Implicit contracts and underemployment equilibria. *Journal of Political Economy*, December 1973, pp. 1183–1202.

M. Baily, Wages and employment under uncertain demand. *Review of Economic Studies*, January 1974, pp. 37–50.

M. Baily, Stabilization policy and private economic behaviour. *Brookings Papers on Economic Activity*, 1978, no. 1, pp. 11–59.

R. Barro, Rational expectations and the role of monetary policy. *Journal of Monetary Economics*, January 1976, pp. 1–31.

R. Barro, Unanticipated money growth and unemployment in the U.S. *American Economic Review*, March 1977a, pp. 101–115.

R. Barro, Long-term contracting, sticky prices and monetary policy. *Journal of Monetary Economics*, July 1977b, pp. 305–316.

R. Barro and S. Fischer, Recent developments in monetary theory. *Journal of Monetary Economics*, April 1976, pp. 133–167.

Board of Governors of the Federal Reserve System, Open market policies and open market procedures. *Staff Studies*, July 1971.

K. Brunner, A scheme for the supply theory of money. *International Economic Review*, January 1961.

K. Brunner, The role of money and monetary policy. *Federal Reserve Bank of St. Louis Review*, July 1968.

K. Brunner, Eine Neuformulierung der Quantitätstheorie des Geldes, die Theorie der relativen Preise, des Geldes, des Outputs und des Beschäftigung. *Kredit und Kapital*, February 1970.

K. Brunner, A survey of selected issues in monetary theory. *Schweizerische Zeitschrift für Volkswirtschaft und Statistik*, 1971, pp. 1–146.

K. Brunner and A. Meltzer, Money, debt and economic activity. *Journal of Political Economy*, September–October 1972, pp. 951–977.

A. Burger, The implementation of monetary policy. *Federal Reserve Bank of St. Louis Review*, March 1971, pp. 20–30.

A. Burger, *The money supply process*, Wadsworth, 1972.

A. Burger, L. Kalish and C. Babb, Money stock control and its implications for money policy. *Federal Reserve Bank of St. Louis Review*, May 1969, pp. 16–24.

Business Week, How expectations defeat economic policy. 7 November 1976, pp. 74–75.

P. Cagan, The monetary dynamics of hyperinflation. In: *Studies in the quantity theory of money*, M. Friedman, ed., Chicago, 1956.

P. Cagan, *Determinants and effects of changes in the stock of money, 1875–1960*, New York, 1965.

J. Carlson, A study of price forecasts. *Annals of Economic and Social Measurement*, 1977, pp. 27–55.

A. Cukierman, Rational expectations and the role of monetary policy: A generalization. *Journal of Monetary Economics*, April 1979, pp. 213–229.

M. Darby, Rational expectations under conditions of costly information. *Journal of Finance*, June 1976, pp. 889–895.

S. DeCanio, Rational expectations and learning from experience. *The Quarterly Journal of Economics*, February 1979, pp. 47–57.

R. Dornbusch, Expectations and exchange rate dynamics. *Journal of Political Economy*, December 1976, pp. 1161–1176.

N. Duck and G. Zis, The natural rate hypothesis, policy rules and fixed exchange rates. *Oxford Economic Papers*, March 1979, pp. 36–46.

D. Duwendag, "The 'new era' of controlling monetary aggregates: Federal Reserve, Swiss National Bank, German Bundesbank". Paper presented at the *Konstanzer Seminar on Monetary Theory and Monetary Policy*, Konstanz, 7–10 June 1977.

J. Evans and G. Yarrow, Adaptive and rational expectations in macro economic models. *The Manchester School of Economic and Social Studies*, March 1979, pp. 24–32.

E. Fama, Efficient capital markets: a review of theoretical and empirical work. *Journal of Finance*, Papers and Proceedings, May 1970, pp. 383–417.

E. Fama, Short term interest rates as predictors of inflation. *American Economic Review*, June 1975, pp. 2569–2582.

B. Faulwasser, Zur Bedeutung von Erwartungen bei Preis-und Mengenreaktionen. *Volkswirtschaftliche Schriften*, Berlin, 1979.

Federal Reserve Bank of Boston, *Controlling monetary aggregates*, Boston, 1969.

Federal Reserve Bank of Minneapolis, *A prescription for monetary policy: proceedings from a seminar series*, Minneapolis, 1976.

Federal Reserve Bank of Minneapolis, Rational expectations: fresh ideas that challenge some established views of policy making, in *Annual report*, Minneapolis, 1977, pp. 1–14.

Federal Reserve Bank of New York, *Monetary aggregates and monetary policy*, New York, 1974.

E. Feige and D. Pearce, Economically rational expectations: Are innovations in the rate of inflation independent of innovations in measures of monetary and fiscal policy? *Journal of Political Economy*, June 1976, pp. 499–522.

S. Fischer, Long-term contracts, rational expectations and the optimal money supply rule. *Journal of Political Economy*, February 1977a.

S. Fischer, Long-term contracting, sticky prices and monetary policy: a comment. *Journal of Monetary Economics*, July 1977b, pp. 317–333.

I. Fisher, A statistical relation between unemployment and price changes. *International Labour Review*, June 1926, pp. 785–792 (Reprinted in *Journal of Political Economy*, March–April 1973, pp. 496–502).

I. Fisher, *The theory of interest*, New York, 1930.

W. Frazer, Evolutionary economics, rational expectations, and monetary policy. *Journal of Economic Issues*, June 1978, pp. 343–372.

J. Frenkel, Inflation and the formation of expectations. *Journal of Monetary Economics*, October 1975, pp. 403–421.

J. Frenkel, The forward exchange rate, expectations and the demand for money: the German hyperinflation. *American Economic Review*, September 1977, pp. 653–675.

J. Frenkel and C. Rodriguez, Notes on output and expectations in the process of inflation. *Weltwirtschaftliches Archiv*, 1977, Heft 3, pp. 423–433.

B. Friedman, Stability and rationality in models of hyperinflation. *International Economic Review*, February 1978, pp. 45–64.

B. Friedman, Optimal expectations and the extreme information assumptions of "rational expectations" macromodels. *Journal of Monetary Economics*, January 1979, pp. 32–41.

M. Friedman, ed., *Studies in the quantity theory of money*. Chicago, 1956.

M. Friedman, The role of monetary policy. *American Economic Review*, March 1968, pp. 1–17.

M. Friedman, The quantity theory of money, a restatement, in *The optimum quantity of money and other essays*, Chicago, Aldine, 1969a, pp. 51–68.

M. Friedman, The role of monetary policy, in *The optimum quantity of money and other essays*, Chicago, 1969b, pp. 95–111.

M. Friedman, *Unemployment versus inflation? An evaluation of the Phillips curve*. IEA Lecture 2, London, Institute of Economic Affairs, 1975a.

M. Friedman, Discussion: rediscovery of money. *American Economic Review*, May 1975b, pp. 176–177.

M. Friedman, *Price theory*, Chicago, 1976.

M. Friedman, Nobel lecture: inflation and unemployment. *Journal of Political Economy*, 1977.

M. Friedman and A. Schwartz, *A monetary history of the United States*, 1867–1960, Princeton, Princeton University Press, 1963.

H. Frisch, Monetarism and monetary economics. *Kredit und Kapital*, 1977a, no. 3, pp. 321–333.

H. Frisch, Inflation theory 1963–1975, a "second generation" survey. *Journal of Economic Literature*, December 1977b, pp. 1289–1317.

W. Gazzard, The new down-to-earth economics. *Fortune*, December 1978.

W. Gibson, Price expectations effects on interest rates. *Journal of Finance*, March 1970, pp. 19–32.

W. Gibson, Interest rates and inflationary expectations: new evidence. *American Economic Review*, December 1972, pp. 854–865.

C. A. Goodhart, *Money, information and uncertainty*, New York, Macmillan 1975.

R. Gordon, Wage-price controls and the shifting Phillips curve. *Brookings Papers on Economic Activity*, 1972, p. 385–421.

R. Gordon, A neo-classical theory of Keynesian unemployment. *Economic Inquiry*, December 1974, pp. 431–459.

R. Gordon, Can econometric policy evaluations be salvaged? A comment. *Journal of Monetary Economics*, January 1976a, pp. 47–62.

R. Gordon, Recent developments in the theory of inflation and unemployment. *Journal of Monetary Economics*, April 1976b, pp. 185–216.

R. Gordon, The theory of domestic inflation. *American Economic Review*, Papers and Proceedings, February 1977, pp. 128–134.

R. Gordon, What can stabilization policy achieve? *American Economic Review*, Papers and Proceedings, May 1978.

B. Grosseschmidt, Kritik der postkeynesianischen Stabilitätspolitik, ein Beitrag zur Phillips-Kurven-Diskussion. *Volkswirtschaftliche Schriften*, 1976, pp. 95–120. Berlin.

F. H. Hahn, Expectations and equilibrium. *Economic Journal*, December 1952.

R. Hall, The rigidity of wages and the persistence of unemployment. *Brookings Papers on Economic Activity*, 1975, no. 2, pp. 301–325.

R. Hall, The Phillips curve and macro-economic policy, in: The Phillips curve and labour markets. *Journal of Monetary Economics*, supplement, 1976.

R. Hall, A theory of the natural unemployment rate and the duration of employment. *Journal of Monetary Economics*, April 1979, pp. 153–169.

D. Heremans, A. Verheirstraten, C. de Poortere, L. Deryck and M. van Hecke, Theorie van de conjunctuurpolitiek, in *Conjunctuurtheorie en conjunctuurpolitiek*, Twaalfde Vlaams Wetenschappelijk Economisch Congres, Gent, 11–12 April 1975, pp. 444–458.

J. R. Hicks, *Value and capital*, Oxford, Clarendon, 1939.

P. Howitt, Activist monetary policy under rational expectations. Discussion paper presented at the Congress of the American Economic Association, 30 December 1977.

T. Humphrey, Some current controversies in the theory of inflation. *Economic Review, Federal Reserve Bank of Richmond*, July–August 1976.

T. Humphrey, Some recent developments in Phillips curve analysis. *Economic Review, Federal Reserve Bank of Richmond*, January–February 1978.

J. Jordan, Elements of money stock determination. *Federal Reserve Bank of St. Louis Review*, October 1969, p. 10–19.

Journal of Monetary Economics, The Phillips curve and labor markets, Supplement, 1976.

Journal of Monetary Economics, The problem of inflation, Supplement, February 1978.

J. Kareken, Inflation, an extreme view. *Federal Reserve Bank of Minneapolis Quarterly Review*, Winter 1978, pp. 1–13.

M. Keran, Selecting a monetary indicator – evidence from the United States and other developed countries. *Federal Reserve Bank of St. Louis Review*, September 1970.

J. M. Keynes, *A treatise on money*, London, 1930.

N. Khan, The variability of expectations in hyperinflations. *Journal of Political Economy*, August 1977, pp. 817–827.

P. Korteweg, *De monetaire sector, het aanbod van geld en de instrumenten van monetaire politiek*, Leiden, 1971.

P. Korteweg, The supply and controllability of money in an open economy, the Dutch case. *De Economist*, 1974, pp. 273–289.

P. Korteweg, Activisme of automatie in de monetaire politiek? *Economisch Statistische Berichten*, 26 May 1976a.

P. Korteweg, Rationeel gedrag en de effectloosheid van anti-cyclische monetaire politiek: een naschrift. *Economisch Statistische Berichten*, 15 December 1976b.

P. Korteweg, Assessment and critical appraisal of the OECD views on economic policy. Paper presented to the first meeting of the Shadow European Economic Policy Committee, Paris, 26–27 May 1977.

P. Korteweg, The economics of inflation and output fluctuations in the Netherlands, 1954–1975: a test of some implications of the dominant impulse-cum-rational expectations hypothesis, in: The problem of inflation. *Journal of Monetary Economics*, supplement, February 1978, pp. 17–80.

P. Korteweg, The economics of stagflation: theory and Dutch evidence, Paper presented at the *Konstanzer Seminar on Monetary Theory and Monetary Policy*, Konstanz, June 1979.

P. Korteweg and E. Bomhoff, Inflatie en produktiegroei in 1977: een monetaristische voorspelling voor Nederland. *Economisch Statistische Berichten*, 18 May 1977.

J. Kuné, Enige ontwikkelingen in de monetaire theorie: een comparatieve literatuurstudie. *Maandschrift Economie*, June–July 1976.

K. Lahiri, Inflationary expectations: their formation and interest rate effects. *American Economic Review*, March 1976, pp. 124–132.

D. Laidler, Expectations and the Phillips curve trade-off: a commentary. *Scottish Journal of Political Economy*, February 1976, pp. 55–74.

D. Laidler, Money and money income: an essay on the "transmission mechanism". *Journal of Monetary Economics*, July 1978, pp. 151–191.

D. Laidler and M. Parkin, Inflation; a survey. *Economic Journal*, December 1975, pp. 770–773.

A. Lerner, The inflationary process, some theoretical aspects. *Review of Economics and Statistics*, August 1949.

R. Lucas, Some international evidence on output-inflation tradeoffs. *American Economic Review*, June 1973, pp. 326–334.

R. Lucas, Econometric policy evaluation: a critique, in: The Phillips curve and labor markets. *Journal of Monetary Economics*, supplement, 1976, pp. 19–43.

B. McCallum, Rational expectations and the natural rate hypothesis. *Econometrica*, January 1976, pp. 43–52.

B. McCallum, Price stickiness and the feasibility of monetary stabilization policy with rational expectations. *Journal of Political Economy*, June 1977, pp. 627–634.

B. McCallum, Price level adjustments and the rational expectations approach to macroeconomic stabilization policy. *Journal of Money, Credit and Banking*, November 1978, pp. 418–436.

B. McCallum and J. Whitaker, The effectiveness of fiscal feedback rules and automatic stabilizers under rational expectations. *Journal of Monetary Economics*, April 1979, pp. 171–186.

A. Marshall, *Money, credit and commerce*, London, 1923.

D. Mathieson, The impact of monetary and fiscal policy under flexible exchange rates and alternative expectations structures. *IMF Staff Papers*, November 1977, pp. 535–568.

A. Meltzer, Controlling money. *Federal Reserve Bank of St. Louis Review*, October 1971, pp. 6–22.

L. von Mises, *Theorie des Geldes*, 1924.

F. Mishkin, Efficient markets theory: implications for monetary policy. *Brookings Papers on Economic Activity*, 1978, no. 4, pp. 707–768.

F. Modigliani, The monetarist controversy or, should we forsake stabilization policies? *American Economic Review*, March 1977, pp. 1–19.

F. Modigliani and R. Shiller, Inflation, rational expectations and the term structure of interest rates. *Economica*, February 1973, pp. 12–43.

D. Mortensen, Job search, the duration of unemployment and the Phillips curve. *American Economic Review*, December 1970, pp. 847–862.

D. Mullineaux, Inflation expectations and money growth in the United States. Research paper 28, *Federal Reserve Bank of Philadelphia*, July 1977a.

D. Mullineaux, Inflation expectations in the U.S.: a brief anatomy. *Federal Reserve Bank of Philadelphia Review*, July–August 1977b, pp. 5–7.

M. Mussa, Adaptive and regressive expectations in a rational model of the inflationary process. *Journal of Monetary Economics*, October 1975, pp. 423–442.

J. Muth, Rational expectations and the theory of price movements. *Econometrica*, July 1961, pp. 315–335.

De Nederlandsche Bank, *Jaarverslag*, 1976.

De Nederlandsche Bank, *Jaarverslag*, 1978.

M. Neldner, The determinants of the currency ratio, the time deposit ratio and the savings deposit ratio: an econometric analysis for the West-German Economy. Paper presented at the *Konstanzer Seminar on Monetary Theory and Monetary Policy*, Konstanz, June 1977.

Newsweek, The new economists, 3 July 1978.

C. K. Nieuwenburg, Een vorm van modern monetarisme. *Maandschrift Economie*, September 1973.

C. K. Nieuwenburg, Geld en economische activiteit, in *Economische theorie en economische politiek in discussie*, Leiden, 1977, pp. 235–273.

A. Okun, Potential G.N.P.: its measurement and significance, *American Statistical Association*, 1962.

A. Okun, Inflation: its mechanics and welfare costs. *Brookings Papers on Economic Activity*, 1975, pp. 351–390.

M. Parkin, *Persistent depression and "stagflation" as consequences of rational expectations and inconsistent policies*, London, 1975.

M. Parkin, The transition from fixed exchange rates to money supply targets. *Journal of Money, Credit and Banking*, February 1977.

M. Parkin, Unemployment and inflation: facts, theories, puzzles and policies. Discussion paper presented at the *Conference of the International Economic Association, Strasbourg*, 28 August–2 September 1978.

B. Pashigiani, Rational expectations and the Cobweb-theory. *Journal of Political Economy*, March–April 1970, pp. 338–355.

J. Pesando, Rational expectations and distributed lag expectations proxies. *Journal of the American Statistical Association*, March 1976, pp. 36–41.

E. Phelps, Phillips curves, expectations of inflation and unemployment over time. *Economica*, August 1967, pp. 254–281.

E. Phelps. *Micro economic foundations of employment and inflation theory*, New York, 1970.

E. Phelps, Macro-equilibrium, inflation expectations and the 'natural' unemployment rate, in *Inflation policy and unemployment theory*, 1972a, pp. 35–58.

E. Phelps, *Inflation policy and unemployment theory*, 1972b.

E. Phelps, Checking contractual inflation without causing recession: adaptive guideposts and monetary strategy. *Konstanzer Seminar on Monetary Theory and Monetary Policy*, Konstanz, June 1977.

E. Phelps and J. Taylor, Stabilizing powers of monetary policy under rational expectations. *Journal of Political Economy*, February 1977, pp. 163–190.

A. Phillips, The relation between unemployment and the rate of change of money wage rates in the United Kingdom, 1861–1957. *Economica*, November 1958, pp. 283–299.

R. Pohl, Akzeptierte Arbeitslosigkeit und dauerhafte Trade-offs. Zur Dichotomie kurzfristiger Anpassungen und langfristiger Gleichgewichtszustände, *Zeitschrift für die Gesamte Staatswissenschaft*, March 1979, pp. 17–40.

W. Poole, Rational expectations in the macro model. *Brookings Papers on Economic Activity*, 1976, no. 2, pp. 436–505.

E. Prescott, Efficiency of the natural rate. *Journal of Political Economy*, 1975, pp. 1229–1236.

H. Ramser, Rationale Erwartungen und Wirtschaftspolitik. *Zeitschrift für die Gesamte Staatswissenschaft*, 1978a, pp. 57–72.

H. Ramser, Die Kontrakttheorie als Beitrag zu einer ökonomischen Theorie des Arbeitsmarktes. *Zeitschrift für die Gesamte Staatswissenschaft*, December 1978b, pp. 628–659.

R. Rasche, A review of empirical studies of the money supply mechanism. *Federal Reserve Bank of St. Louis Review*, July 1972, pp 11–19.

J. Rutledge, *A monetarist model of inflationary expectations*, Lexington, 1974.

J. Rutledge, Irving Fisher and auto-regressive expectations. *American Economic Review*, Papers and Proceedings, February 1977, pp. 200–205.

P. Samuelson, The role of money in national economic policy, in *Controlling monetary aggregates*, Boston, Federal Reserve Bank of Boston, 1969.

A. Santomoro and J. Seater, The inflation-unemployment trade-off: a critique of the literature. *Journal of Economic Literature*, June 1978, pp. 499–544.

T. Sargent, A note on the "accelerationist" controversy. *Journal of Money, Credit and Banking*, August 1971, pp. 721–725.

T. Sargent, Rational expectations and the term structure of interest rates. *Journal of Money, Credit and Banking*, February 1972.

T. Sargent, Rational expectations, the real rate of interest and the natural rate of unemployment. *Brookings Papers on Economic Activity*, 1973, no. 2.

T. Sargent and N. Wallace, Rational expectations, the optimal monetary instrument and the optimal money supply rule. *Journal of Political Economy*, April 1975, pp. 241–255.

T. Sargent and N. Wallace, Rational expectations and the theory of economic policy. *Journal of Monetary Economics*, April 1976, pp. 169–183.

W. Scarth, Expectations and the wage–price spiral in a simple monetary model. *Manchester School of Economics and Social Studies*, 1977, pp. 208–219.

K. Schlesinger, Recent experiences with monetary policy in the Federal Republic of Germany. Paper presented at the *Konstanzer Seminar on Monetary Theory and Monetary Policy*, Konstanz, June 1976.

R. Shiller, Rational expectations and the dynamic structure of macro-economic models, a critical review. *Journal of Monetary Economics*, January 1978, pp. 1–44.

J. Siebke and M. Willms, Zinsniveau, Geldpolitik und Inflation. *Kredit und Kapital*, 1972, no. 2, pp. 171–205.

J. Sijben, *Money and economic growth*, Tilburg Studies in Economics, Leiden, Martinus Nijhoff Social Sciences Division, 1978.

J. Sijben, Theoretical foundations of monetary policy: a monetarist view in *New approaches in monetary policy*, Publication of SUERF, Alphen aan den Rijn, Sijthoff & Noordhoff, 1979.

H. Simons, Rules vs. authorities in monetary policy. *Journal of Political Economy*, February 1936, pp. 1–30.

E. Tanner, Indicators of monetary policy: an evaluation of five. *Banca Nazionale del Lavoro Quarterly Review*, December 1972, pp. 413–427.

J. Taylor, Monetary policy during a transition to rational expectations. *Journal of Political Economy*, October 1975, pp. 1009–1021.

J. Tobin, Liquidity preference as behavior towards risk. *Review of Economic Studies*, February 1958.

J. Tobin, Money, capital and other stores of value. *American Economic Review*, May 1961, pp. 26–37.

J. Tobin, Inflation and unemployment. *American Economic Review*, March 1972, pp. 1–18.

J. Trevithick, Inflation, the natural unemployment rate and the theory of economic policy. *Scottish Journal of Political Economy*, February 1976, pp. 37–54.

S. Turnovsky and M. Wachter, A test of the expectations hypothesis using directly observed wage and price expectations. *Review of Economics and Statistics*, 1972, pp. 47–54.

M. Ulmer, Old and new fashions in employment and inflation theory. *Journal of Economic Issues*, March 1979, pp. 1–18.

N. Wallace, Micro-economic theories of macro-economic phenomena and their implications for monetary policy, in: *A prescription for monetary policy: proceedings from a seminar series*. Minneapolis, Federal Reserve Bank of Minneapolis, 1976, pp. 87–98.

K. Wallis, *Econometric implications of the rational expectations hypothesis*, Vienna, 1977.

A. Walters, Consistent expectations, distributed lags and the quantity theory. *Economic Journal*, June 1971, pp. 273–281.

M. Willms, Ende der Konjunkturpolitik, in: Rationale Erwartungen und Stabilitätspolitik. *Wirtschaftsdienst*, 1977, no. 2, pp. 65–67.

G. Woglom, Rational expectations and monetary policy in a simple macro-economic model. *The Quarterly Journal of Economics*, February 1979, pp. 91–105.

A. Woll, Keine neue Revolution in Sicht, in: Rationale Erwartungen und Stabilitätspolitik. *Wirtschaftsdienst*, 1977, no. 2, pp. 59–63.

W. Yohe and D. Karnosky, Interest rates and price level changes, 1952–1969. *Federal Reserve Bank of St. Louis Review*, December 1969, pp. 18–26.

J. Zijlstra, Monetary theory and monetary policy. *De Economist*, 1979, *no*. 1.

Index

About the author

Jac J. Sijben (1939) is Associate-Professor of Monetary Economics in the Economics Faculty of Tilburg University, Tilburg, The Netherlands.

He was educated at Tilburg University where he received his doctorate in 1974. Among his contributions to monetary economics are "Near-banking and monetary policy" (1973), "Money and Economic Activity" (1975) and "Theoretical foundations of monetary policy: a monetarist view" (1979). He is the author of the book *Money and Economic Growth* (1977).

letter: Times New Roman, 11/13, 9/11
setter: Eta Services (Typesetters) Ltd, Common Lane North, Beccles, Suffolk, England
printer: Samsom Sijthoff Grafische Bedrijven
binder: binderij Callenbach
cover-design: W. Bottenheft